BUDDHA BOWLS

TANJA DUSY

BUDDHABOWLS

GRUB STREET • LONDON

CONTENTS

SUPER BOWLS

ALL IN ONE BOWL

The taste of happiness is a colourful bowl filled with delicious, healthy and filling ingredients. The reason why these now popular meals are often called Buddha Bowls may be because as we eat them, they give us a smile of bliss and contentment that we know from depictions of the Buddha.

The idea for them comes from Asia. Many countries there are famous for their traditional one-bowl meals, such as the herb-filled Vietnamese noodle bowls, Korean bibimbap and Japanese chirashi sushi with its toppings pleasantly arranged on a bed of vinegared rice instead of in a roll. They all have one simple and basic concept in common: a selection of different ingredients and flavours are harmoniously combined in the one bowl.

All the dishes in this book share this basic concept. A grain – rice, for example – is combined with a series of versatile and complementary toppings, which can include raw and cooked, sour, spicy and mild ingredients, and thick and runny sauces or dips, among others.

You can start your day with a sweet and filling smoothie in a bowl, or a hearty bowl of millet with roasted tomatoes. A simple bowl of rice noodles with prawns or a vegetarian version with tofu, or a luscious bowl of rice with chickpeas, different vegetables and salad leaves with a delicious sauce can be perfect for lunch or dinner.

Every meal is balanced and enjoyable. And the feeling of contentment lasts: you remain pleasantly full and have more energy long after the meal. When done right, every bowl contains all the essential nutrients we need every day. Now there's no need to rack your brains, whether you're on a vegetarian or low-carb diet, and you definitely don't have to count calories. Each bowl in this book is presented as the most ideal combination possible. Feel free to add what you like or to substitute any of the ingredients with others, so you can feel sated, happy and completely satisfied in your own particular way.

BUDDHA BOWLS –
ALL IN ONE

HEALTHY AND BALANCED

Everything our body needs fits in one bowl, provided we make an intelligent choice, the way the recipes in this book have been put together. They're a combination of the most complex carbohydrates, proteins – fish or plant-based – and lots of vitamins, minerals and phytochemical compounds from fresh greens. The perfect mixture to stay slim and healthy, and a delicious way to stay full longer.

Vegetables and the occasional fruits make up about 50 per cent of each bowl, whether as cooked or raw vegetables or salad leaves. Carbohydrates, in the form of grains or pulses, and protein in the form of fish, dairy or soya products, each make up about 20–25 per cent. The remaining 10 per cent or so comprises high-quality oils, nuts and seeds to give us the amount of fat we need in a healthy way.

By keeping to this principle, you can put together lots of new bowls and modify the recipes in the book by swapping the ingredients for others. Suggestions and further information are provided on pages 10–13.

MIX IT UP!

Mixing and substituting are allowed, even encouraged. If you prefer a vegetarian option, you can replace any fish with tofu or lentils, for instance. Allergy sufferers can use gluten-free quinoa instead of rice. And if you can't be bothered cooking vegetables, mix in a handful of grated carrots and sprinkle a handful of chopped nuts over the top. The only limit is your own imagination. The recipes are designed with practicality in mind, with the main components separated in the ingredient list, and tips include quick options and more complex versions. However, it's important and useful – particularly when it comes to vegetables and fruits – to choose seasonal varieties if possible. The combinations in the recipes always take this into consideration.

There's even more variety thanks to the practical basic recipes provided, which show you how to make popular toppings. Three different ways to prepare sweet potatoes, beetroot, etc. and other special creations make each bowl a unique experience. Although the basic recipes are mixed in with the other recipes in this book, they're highlighted in colour in the table of contents.

UNITY IN DIVERSITY

Another point to consider is the combination of complementary and contrasting flavours and textures. Each bowl should be varied with the right proportion of fresh and cooked ingredients, creamy sauces and hot, sweet and bitter foods. This is done almost instinctively in Asian cuisines. The balance of different flavours is also the basic principle of ancient forms of medicine, such as traditional Chinese medicine and Indian Ayurvedic medicine, which aim to bring balance to body and mind alike. But don't worry; there's no need for you to study them to know that the more often you treat yourself to these bowls, the more you notice how good these colourful combinations are for you. There's also an incomparable pleasure to be found in cooling the heat of a bean chilli with a creamy yoghurt dip, crunching on nuts, and tickling the palate with a little lemon before immediately soothing it with the sweetness of mango. I hope you enjoy your food adventure!

A LOT TO GAIN FROM A LITTLE EFFORT

Admittedly, bowls do require some effort. In return, however, you get a healthy, balanced and filling meal with the added feeling of satisfaction. You should therefore not be put off when you see a list of four or five components. If you find it really stressing, just leave one out or take a short cut, for instance, by substituting the chickpea curry with plain chickpeas straight from the tin, or by simply adding chopped up salad leaves instead of making a salad and dressing. At the same time, the recipes are designed for convenient time management. For instance, there are lots of dishes where the main part of the work is done by the oven, letting you chop raw vegetables, cook rice or stir-fry other vegetables in the meantime. And if you have leftover pickles (see p. 40) in the fridge, that means there's less work for you and less of your time and effort are required.

 The quantities given in the recipes are enough to make two bowls.

 All oven cooking and temperatures require top and bottom heat.

KEY

  VEGETARIAN   FISH

 VEGAN

HEALTHY CARBOHYDRATES

These form the basic component of each bowl as our body and our brain, in particular, need carbohydrates. Complex carbohydrates are better for us as they are broken down very gradually by our body and only very slowly raise our blood sugar levels, unlike simple carbohydrates, such as sugar, which give us a short rush of energy before we crash and feel hungry again. That's why it's better to eat whole foods that are high in fibre, which will keep you full and satisfied for a long time.

IDEAL CARBOHYDRATES

Neutral and good: rice or noodles; it's even better to use brown rice, a wild rice mix and red rice

Quick and uncomplicated: bulgur, couscous and durum wheat (Ebly®)

Wholegrains and seeds: oats, wheat, spelt, barley, quinoa and amaranth (the last two being gluten-free)

LEAF VEGETABLES

Leaf vegetables are packed with nutrients and provide crunch and a pleasant texture when eaten raw; the perfect complement for cooked vegetables

Small and fine: baby spinach, baby chard, pak choi, Chinese mustard leaves and other baby salad leaves – available packaged in the fresh food section of most supermarkets

Fresh and high in vitamins: cress (or other sprouts sold growing in punnets, such as radish, broccoli, rocket, alfalfa, mung bean, pea; available in the fresh food section of supermarkets)

Spring fresh: purslane and watercress (available in bunches)

Simple salad leaves: all fresh varieties, such as Lollo Rosso and cos lettuce, lamb's lettuce, rocket, radicchio and endive

VEGETABLES AND FRUIT

The amount of carbohydrates varies depending on the variety, but they always contain vitamins, minerals and phytochemical compounds that are essential for health and fitness. Raw or slightly cooked to preserve as many as possible. Vegetables that are high in carbohydrates are often identified by their sweetish taste and become 'floury' when cooked (owing to their high starch content).

Spring: asparagus, carrots, peas, kohlrabi, pointed cabbage, radishes, spinach, spring onions

Summer: tomatoes, peppers, cucumbers, aubergines, courgettes, broccoli, cauliflower, daikon radish, beans, Swiss chard, fennel

Autumn pumpkin and winter squash, celery, leeks, maincrop spinach, sweetcorn

Winter beetroot, sweet potatoes, cabbage (red cabbage, white cabbage, kale, cavolo nero, Savoy cabbage, Brussels sprouts, pak choi)

Also: mushrooms (button mushrooms, oyster mushrooms) and sea vegetables, i.e. (dried) seaweeds

Easy options from the cupboard: pickled vegetables

HEALTHY PROTEINS

Proteins are essential building blocks for muscle, bones and blood vessels, even blood, without which we wouldn't be able to exist. They can be sourced from both fish and plants. A combination of both types of proteins, which are complementary, is particularly advantageous.

ANIMAL-BASED PROTEINS

Fish: if possible from certified, sustainable fisheries (look for the MSC seal) or farmed fish – oily fish rich in healthy omega fatty acids, such as mackerel and salmon, are ideal.

Seafood: prawns, crabs, squid, mussels

Eggs

Dairy products: cheese, including cream cheese, yoghurt and quark – not only made from cow's milk, but also from goat's milk and ewe's milk

PLANT-BASED PROTEINS

Soya-based products: tofu, tempeh and miso paste

Legume-based: soya beans (dried or fresh as edamame), beans, lentils, peas

Nuts and seeds

Grains: Quinoa, amaranth, buckwheat and millet

HEALTHY FATS

First of all, fat doesn't actually make us fat; it ensures that our body runs like clockwork: It's a good source of energy and healthy fatty acids, and it helps our bodies to absorb certain vitamins. In particular, the omega-3 fatty acids found in certain seeds, oily fish, eggs and avocado are the best medicine to fight against unhealthy lipids known as bad cholesterol.

GOOD FATS

Cold-pressed oils: olive oil, rapeseed oil, linseed oil

Coconut oil contains plenty of saturated fat, but in the form of healthy MCT fatty acids, which the body doesn't store as fat cells

Olives

Nuts and seeds

Avocados

Oily fish: such as salmon and mackerel

BREAKFAST

BOWLS

CHIA PUDDING BOWL

INGREDIENTS

125 g raspberries

⅓ vanilla pod

350 ml almond milk

4 tbsp chia seeds

125 g blackberries or blueberries

3 tbsp flaked almonds

2 tbsp coconut chips

2 tbsp agave syrup (substitute with maple syrup)

HERE'S WHAT TO DO

1 Carefully wash 100 g of raspberries. Split the vanilla pod along its length with a knife and scrape out the seeds. Blend the raspberries with the vanilla seeds and almond milk and put into a glass jar with an airtight lid. Add the chia seeds and stir very well. Stir well again after about 10–20 minutes to break up any clumps. Close the jar and leave the seeds to swell overnight in the refrigerator.

2 The next day, carefully wash the remaining raspberries and the blackberries or blueberries and pat dry with kitchen paper. Toast the flaked almonds in a dry frying pan until light golden. Then remove from the heat and leave to cool. Fill bowls with the chia pudding and scatter over with berries, flaked almonds and coconut chips. Sweeten with agave syrup.

 **LAZY MORNING**

This bowl is also ideal for when you're on the go: Simply put a serving of the chia pudding in a screw-lid jar and pack the berries, flaked almonds and coconut chips in separate bags.

When you're ready, put everything together for a stress-free start to your day.

VEGAN

APPLE AND CARROT BOWL

INGREDIENTS

FOR THE APPLE COMPOTE

2 small apples (about 200 g)

1 tsp lemon juice

¼ cinnamon stick

1–2 tbsp honey

50 ml apple juice

FOR THE CARROT SALAD

1 large, thick carrot

1 tbsp dried cranberries

1 tsp lemon juice

1 tsp almond oil (substitute with sunflower oil)

1 tsp honey

FOR THE COUSCOUS

125 g couscous

Salt

1 tsp butter (substitute with sunflower oil)

EXTRAS

4 tbsp flaked hazelnuts

½–¾ tsp ground cinnamon

HERE'S WHAT TO DO

1 For the compote, peel, quarter and core the apples. Cut into small dice. Mix them immediately with the lemon juice and the remaining ingredients in a pan and heat. Cook over a medium–low heat, covered, for 20–25 minutes without fully boiling the apples. Take out the cinnamon stick.

2 Peel, wash and coarsely grate the carrots. Coarsely chop the cranberries. Mix together the lemon juice, oil and honey and then mix with the carrots and cranberries.

3 Put the couscous in a small pan, add a pinch of salt and pour over 125 ml of boiling water. Put the pan over a low heat and leave to swell for about 5 minutes. Mix in the butter (or oil) and leave for 5 more minutes.

4 In the meantime, toast the flaked hazelnuts in a dry frying pan and then leave to cool.

5 Fill bowls with couscous and top with apple compote and carrot salad. Scatter over flaked hazelnuts and, optionally, sprinkle with cinnamon as desired.

BEJEWELLED BOWL

INGREDIENTS

FOR THE QUARK

8 dried figs

1 organic orange

1 star anise

⅓ cinnamon stick

250 g quark (40% fat)

2 pinches grated organic
  lemon zest

1 tbsp runny honey

2 tbsp pistachio nuts

EXTRAS

80 g coarse oatmeal

Salt

3 tbsp shelled walnuts

1 persimmon

3 tbsp pomegranate seeds

HERE'S WHAT TO DO

1 Cut the figs into pieces. Wash and dry the orange, finely grate the zest and squeeze the juice. Combine the juice with 2 pinches of the grated zest and the spices in a small saucepan and bring to the boil. Add the figs, lower the heat and simmer, uncovered, for 15 minutes. Leave to cool a little and take out the spices. Cool until lukewarm.

2 Mix the quark with the lemon zest and honey until smooth. Coarsely chop the pistachios and stir most of them into the mixture.

3 Bring 450 ml of water to the boil in a small saucepan. Mix in the oatmeal and, stirring constantly, bring back to the boil. Then reduce the heat to low. Cover with a lid and simmer gently for 10 minutes, stirring occasionally to prevent the porridge from sticking to the bottom. Finally, season with a little salt.

4 Meanwhile, coarsely chop the walnuts. Wash and slice the persimmon crossways and cut off the top.

5 Fill bowls with porridge and arrange persimmon slices on top. Put some quark next to them and spread some of the figs and their liquid over the quark and porridge. Scatter the remaining chopped pistachios over the top. Finish with pomegranate seeds and chopped walnuts.

VEGETARIAN

VEGAN

TROPICAL COCONUT BOWL

INGREDIENTS

FOR THE COCONUT RICE

½ vanilla pod

400 ml coconut milk

180 g pudding rice

2 tbsp demerara sugar

2–3 tbsp lime juice

FOR THE MANGO COMPOTE

1 ripe mango (about 400 g)

¼ vanilla pod

2 tbsp demerara sugar

150 ml freshly squeezed mandarin juice

2 tbsp lime juice

EXTRAS

½ papaya

3 tbsp desiccated coconut

Small mint leaves to garnish

HERE'S WHAT TO DO

1 Split the vanilla pod along its length with a knife and scrape out the seeds. Combine the pod and seeds with the coconut milk in a pan and bring to the boil. Add the rice and sugar, cover with a lid and cook over a low heat for 20–25 minutes, until the rice swells. Towards the end of this time, season with the lime juice. Take out the vanilla pod.

2 In the meantime, make the compote. Peel the mango, remove the flesh by cutting diagonally to the stone and finely dice. Split the vanilla pod and scrape out the seeds. Combine the pod and seeds with the sugar, mandarin juice and lime juice in a pan and bring to the boil. Reduce the heat to low and simmer, uncovered, for 15 minutes. Add the mango dice to the pan and simmer for 3–5 minutes. Then remove from the heat and leave to cool until lukewarm.

3 Peel the papaya, remove the seeds and cut the flesh into slices. Toast the desiccated coconut in a dry frying pan until it releases its aroma and begins to turn golden. Then remove from the heat and leave to cool. Wash the mint leaves and pat dry with kitchen paper. Optionally, they can be finely chopped.

4 Fill bowls with coconut rice, top with mango compote and papaya slices and sprinkle with desiccated coconut. Garnish with mint leaves.

BANANA AND CHOCOLATE BOWL

INGREDIENTS

FOR THE SMOOTHIE
4 bananas

100–120 ml almond milk

1½ tbsp peanut butter

3 tsp cocoa powder

1 tbsp cocoa nibs

FOR THE TOPPING
1 tbsp pumpkin seeds

2 tbsp pecan nuts

1 tsp chia seeds

1 tbsp cocoa nibs

1 tbsp bee pollen

4 tbsp blueberries

2 tbsp blackberries

HERE'S WHAT TO DO

1 Peel and slice the bananas. Freeze for at least 4 hours or overnight.

2 For the topping, toast the pumpkin seeds in a frying pan until they crackle and release their aroma. Then remove from the heat and leave to cool. Coarsely chop the pecans and mix with the chia seeds, cocoa nibs and pollen. Wash the berries and pat dry with kitchen paper.

3 Combine the frozen banana slices with 100 ml almond milk, the peanut butter, cocoa powder and cocoa nibs in a high-speed blender and blend until very smooth. Add a little more almond milk if necessary.

4 Fill two bowls with the smoothie and sprinkle with berries and the nut, seed and pollen mixture.

 ## SUBSTITUTING

This recipe provides a suggestion for a balanced, tasty and healthy topping, but if you don't have or don't like certain ingredients, you can naturally substitute them with others. Good alternatives are linseed (preferably golden), hemp seeds, walnuts, hazelnuts and almonds.

VEGAN

VEGAN

GREEN SMOOTHIE BOWL

INGREDIENTS

FOR THE SMOOTHIE

150 g kale leaves

120 g spinach

Juice of 3 oranges

2 apples

5 dried dates (preferably
   Medjool)

EXTRAS

125 g raspberries

6 tbsp granola (shop-
   bought or see tip)

HERE'S WHAT TO DO

1 Wash and finely chop the kale and spinach leaves. Halve
   and squeeze the oranges. Wash, halve and core the apples and cut into chunks. Pit and finely chop the dates.
   Combine the ingredients in a (preferably high-speed)
   blender and blend until very smooth.

2 Fill bowls with the smoothie. Clean or carefully wash the
   berries and pat dry with kitchen paper. Scatter them over
   the smoothie. Finally, sprinkle with granola.

 ### HOME-MADE GRANOLA

Coarsely chop or halve 100 g of hazelnuts and mix with 180 g
of cereal flakes (e.g. spelt, oats or multigrain); 30 g each of sesame seeds, pumpkin seeds and sunflower seeds; and 40 g
desiccated coconut. Sprinkle with 1 teaspoon of ground cinnamon. Add 5 tablespoons of runny honey or maple syrup
and 4 tablespoons of sunflower oil and mix everything well
with your hands or a spoon until the mixture is really sticky.
Spread the mixture out evenly on a baking tray lined with
baking parchment. Bake in the oven (middle shelf) at 180°C
(160°C fan) for 20–25 minutes until dark golden, stirring once
or twice if necessary. Take the tray out of the oven and leave
to allow the granola to cool down completely. Store it in an
airtight jar and use it as a topping for smoothies, to make
muesli and with yoghurt.

PURPLE SUPERFOOD BOWL

INGREDIENTS

FOR THE SMOOTHIE

1 ripe mango (about 380 g)

60 g each frozen raspberries
and blackberries

100 g frozen açai purée
(from organic food shops)

Juice of 1 orange

FOR THE TOPPING

125 g blueberries

1 small banana

2 tbsp dried cranberries

2 tbsp goji berries

HERE'S WHAT TO DO

1 Peel the mango and cut away the flesh from around the
stone. Coarsely dice and combine with the frozen berries
in a blender. Break up the frozen açai purée and add it to
the blender with the orange juice. Blend until very smooth.

2 In the meantime, prepare the topping. Wash the blueberries and pat dry with kitchen paper. Peel and slice
the banana.

3 Fill bowls with the smoothie. Top with banana slices,
blueberries, cranberries and goji berries.

 SUBSTITUTING

Instead of the topping included here, the home-made nut
crunch (see p. 33) also works well with the açai smoothie.

VEGAN

VEGAN

NO SALAD BOWL

INGREDIENTS

FOR THE SMOOTHIE
180 g organic cucumber

1 ripe avocado

3 tbsp lime juice

80 g baby spinach

120 g cos lettuce

1 ½ tbsp peanut butter

½ tsp ground cumin

Salt and pepper

FOR THE TOPPING
50 g radish sprouts

125 g cherry tomatoes in assorted colours

1 tbsp each black and white sesame seeds

1 tbsp pumpkin seeds

1 tbsp sunflower seeds

2 pinches chilli flakes (optional)

HERE'S WHAT TO DO

1 Wash and cut the cucumber into pieces. Halve and stone the avocado and scoop out the flesh with a spoon. Mix it immediately with the lime juice and combine with the cucumber in a blender. Wash the spinach and lettuce leaves. Shake dry and cut them into small pieces. Add them to the blender together with the peanut butter. Add the cumin and 180–200 ml of water and blend until very smooth. Season with salt and pepper.

2 For the topping, put the radish sprouts into a sieve, wash under cold water, drain and pat dry with kitchen paper. Wash and remove the stems from the tomatoes. Cut into halves or quarters. Toast the sesame seeds, pumpkin seeds and sunflower seeds in a dry frying pan until they crackle and release their aroma. Then remove from the heat and leave to cool.

3 Fill bowls with the smoothie, add the tomatoes and sprouts and sprinkle with the seed mixture. Optionally, sprinkle with chilli flakes.

 SUBSTITUTING

Instead of the seed mixture, sprinkle the bowl with dukkah (see p. 32).

CRISPY TOPPINGS

DUKKAH

INGREDIENTS

80 g hazelnuts

2 tbsp pine nuts

2 tbsp sesame seeds

1 tbsp cumin

2 tbsp coriander seeds

½ tsp nigella seeds

½ tsp coarse sea salt

¾ tsp dried oregano

2 tsp sweet paprika

½ tsp freshly ground black pepper

HERE'S WHAT TO DO

1 Heat the oven to 160°C (fan not recommended). Put the hazelnuts on a baking tray and roast in the oven (middle shelf) for 15–20 minutes, until golden. Add the pine nuts after 10 minutes. Then take them out and leave to cool.

2 Toast the sesame seeds in a dry non-stick frying pan until they turn golden and start to crackle. Then remove from the heat. Next, toast the cumin and coriander seeds until they release their aroma.

3 Coarsely chop the hot pine nuts and sesame seeds. Then transfer to a container and leave to cool.

4 Rub the hazelnuts between your hands to remove their skins. Then combine with the toasted spices, nigella seeds, salt and oregano in a mortar and coarsely crush. Mix with the paprika, pepper, pine nuts and sesame seeds.

 TIP

Dukkah is an Egyptian spice mix that is traditionally served with flat bread. Typically, a piece of the bread is torn off, dipped in olive oil and then in the spice mix. But it is also delicious when sprinkled over salads, raw vegetables and vegetable bowls, or over pulses, such as chickpeas.

SPICY GRANOLA

INGREDIENTS

200 g blanched almonds

100 g cashew nuts

100 g pecan nuts

50 g sunflower seeds

1 tbsp honey

1 tbsp demerara sugar

1½ tbsp sunflower oil

¾ tsp sea salt

1 tsp garam masala

⅓ tsp chilli powder

HERE'S WHAT TO DO

1   Heat the oven to 180°C (160°C fan). Spread the almonds, cashews, pecans and sunflower seeds out on a baking tray lined with baking parchment and roast in the oven (middle shelf) for about 5 minutes. Put the honey, sugar and oil in a non-stick frying pan over a medium heat and stir to combine. Stir in the salt and spices.

2   Take the nuts and seeds out of the oven, add the spice mixture and stir until evenly coated. Return the nuts and seeds to the baking tray and roast for 10 more minutes. Take out of the oven and leave to cool. Store in an airtight jar.

 TIP

Whether whole or coarsely chopped, nuts make a great topping to sprinkle over bowls, but they also make a good snack.

NUT CRUNCH

INGREDIENTS

70 g almonds

50 g hazelnuts

50 g shelled walnuts

2 tbsp hemp seeds

2 tbsp chia seeds

2 tbsp cocoa nibs

6 dried dates

¾ tsp gingerbread spice mix

HERE'S WHAT TO DO

1   Heat the oven to 160°C. Spread the almonds and hazelnuts out on a baking tray and roast for 15–20 minutes until golden. Add the walnuts after 10 minutes. Then take them out and leave to cool.

2   Rub the hazelnuts between your hands to remove their skins. Coarsely chop all the nuts and mix them with the hemp seeds, chia seeds and cocoa nibs. Pit and finely chop the dates. Sprinkle them with the gingerbread spice mix and press lightly so the spices adhere. Then mix the dates into the nut mixture. Store the nut crunch in an airtight jar and use as a topping for (smoothie) bowls and porridge, or add to muesli and fruit salad.

VEGETARIAN

MEDITERRANEAN TOMATO BOWL

INGREDIENTS

FOR THE TOMATOES

400 g cherry tomatoes (assorted colours)

3 sprigs basil

1½ tbsp olive oil

Sea salt, pepper

FOR THE LEMON RICOTTA

½ organic lemon

3 sprigs thyme

2 sprigs basil

250 g soft ricotta cheese

Salt and pepper

2 tbsp olive oil

EXTRAS

100 g millet

1 bunch rocket

2 tbsp roasted and salted almonds

HERE'S WHAT TO DO

1 Cook the millet according to the instructions on the packet and leave to swell. In the meantime, wash and shake dry the rocket and cut off any tough stems. Tear the leaves into small pieces. Coarsely chop the almonds.

2 For the lemon ricotta, wash and dry the lemon, finely grate the zest and squeeze the juice. Wash and shake dry the thyme and basil. Pluck and finely chop the leaves. Mix the cheese with 3 pinches of lemon zest, 2 tablespoons of lemon juice and the herbs. Season with salt and pepper.

3 Wash and dry the tomatoes. Wash and shake dry the basil and pluck and cut the leaves into strips. Heat the olive oil in a non-stick frying pan and fry the tomatoes over a high heat for about 3 minutes, until they begin to burst open and dark patches appear. Season with salt and pepper and stir in the basil.

4 Fill bowls with millet and scatter over the rocket and tomatoes. Add a thick dollop of the lemon ricotta. Drizzle the ricotta with olive oil. Sprinkle the bowls with almonds.

EASY
BOWLS

SPRING BOWL

INGREDIENTS

FOR THE ASPARAGUS

300 g green asparagus spears

2 tbsp olive oil

Grated zest of
⅓ organic lemon

Sugar

FOR THE PEAS

3 spring onions

1 tbsp olive oil

200 g frozen peas

100 ml vegetable stock

1 sprig tarragon

1–2 dash(es) lemon juice

FOR THE TOPPING

1 tbsp apple cider vinegar

2 fresh eggs

1 handful purslane (substitute
with baby spinach)

8 radishes or
pink pickled radish
(see p. 41)

EXTRAS

150 g red quinoa

Salt and pepper

HERE'S WHAT TO DO

1 Heat the oven to 200°C (180°C fan). Wash the asparagus and cut off or peel the woody ends. If necessary, halve any very thick spears lengthways. Lay the asparagus spears side by side on a sheet of aluminium foil. Drizzle the asparagus with olive oil and sprinkle with the lemon zest, salt, pepper and 3 pinches of sugar. Fold the aluminium foil around the asparagus to form a parcel, closing securely, and place on a baking tray. Cook in the oven (middle shelf) for about 30 minutes.

2 In the meantime, rinse the quinoa in a sieve with boiling water. Bring 300 ml of salted water to the boil, add the quinoa and cook, covered, over a low heat for 25 minutes. Wash, sort and spin dry the purslane. Wash, trim and slice the radishes.

3 Prepare the peas. Wash, trim and slice the spring onions, both green and white parts, into rings. Heat the olive oil in a pan and sauté the white spring onion rings. Add the peas, pour in the stock and season with salt and pepper. Cover with a lid and cook over a medium heat for 20 minutes. Wash and finely chop the tarragon and finally stir it into the peas together with the green spring onion rings. Season with lemon juice.

4 For the eggs, fill a pan with 1.5 litres of water, and add the vinegar and bring to the boil. Carefully break each egg into a cup. Turn the heat down to low and, one at a time, gently slide the eggs into the simmering water. Cook for 4–5 minutes and take them out with a skimmer.

5 Fill bowls with the quinoa. Top with asparagus, together with its cooking liquid, pea and spring onion mixture, purslane and either radishes or pickled radish. Arrange a poached egg on top, lightly season with salt and pepper, and serve.

VEGETARIAN

PICKLES

JAPANESE-STYLE PICKLES

INGREDIENTS

1 carrot

100 g daikon radish

100 g organic cucumber

1 piece ginger (10 g)

2–3 pinches chilli flakes

¾ tsp salt

½ tsp sugar

2 tbsp rice vinegar

HERE'S WHAT TO DO

1 Peel and cut the carrot and radish into julienne strips or slices. Wash the cucumber and thinly slice along its length. Cut the slices lengthways into narrow strips and discard the soft inner part containing the seeds. Peel and finely dice the ginger.

2 Combine all the ingredients in a bowl and knead together with your hands. Put a plate on top of the vegetables and press down, then place a heavy tin on top and leave to steep for at least 12 hours. Mix well before serving and drain the pickles before use. Store any leftover pickles in an airtight jar in the refrigerator. They will keep for 2–3 more days.

PINK PICKLED RADISH

INGREDIENTS

150 ml white wine vinegar or apple cider vinegar

2 tbsp sugar

1 beetroot (vacuum-packed)

¾ tsp salt

½ tsp each yellow mustard seeds and white pepper-corns

200 g radishes

HERE'S WHAT TO DO

1 Heat the vinegar and sugar in a saucepan, stirring to dissolve the sugar. Halve or quarter the beetroot. Add the salt, mustard seeds and beetroot, remove from the heat and leave to cool.

2 Wash and thinly slice the radishes. Put them into a screw-lid jar and pour over the pickling liquid together with the beetroot (for colour). Lightly tap the jar against the work surface to release any trapped air bubbles and close with the lid. Leave the radishes to steep for at least 1 week. They will keep for 6 months unopened.

PICKLED ONION RINGS

INGREDIENTS

1 red onion

½ tsp demerara sugar

½ tsp sea salt

180 ml white wine vinegar

¼ tsp peppercorns

5 juniper berries

2 sprigs thyme

HERE'S WHAT TO DO

1 Peel and slice the onion into rings. Bring 300 ml of water to the boil in a small saucepan. Remove from the heat and add the onion rings. Then pour off the water and leave to drain in a sieve.

2 In the meantime, heat the sugar, salt and vinegar with the spices in a saucepan, stirring to dissolve the sugar. Leave to cool until lukewarm. Wash the thyme and shake dry. Put the onion and thyme into a jar and pour the pickling mixture over the top. Close the jar and leave to cool. Leave to steep for 1 day. Unopened, the pickles can be stored in the refrigerator for several weeks.

SUMMER BOWL

INGREDIENTS

FOR THE SALSA

1 large beefsteak tomato

2 sprigs basil

½ clove garlic

1 tsp balsamic vinegar

FOR THE ALMOND SAUCE

50 ml vegetable stock

40 g sun-dried tomatoes in oil

20 g almond butter

Chilli flakes

FOR THE VEGETABLES

1 courgette

1 yellow pepper and 1 red pepper

½ clove garlic

6 sprigs thyme

2–4 tbsp olive oil

EXTRAS

160 g fregola pasta (substitute with kritharaki pasta or small durum wheat noodles, e.g. elbow macaroni)

6 mini mozzarella balls

2 tbsp small black olives

2 tbsp caperberries

Salt and pepper

HERE'S WHAT TO DO

1   For the salsa, wash and remove the stem from the tomato and cut into small dice. Wash and shake dry the basil and pluck and coarsely chop the leaves. Peel and finely chop the garlic. Mix the tomato with the basil, garlic, and season with salt, pepper and the vinegar and leave to marinate. Pat dry and halve or quarter the mozzarella balls.

2   In the meantime, make the almond sauce. Heat the vegetable stock and coarsely chop the dried tomatoes. Blend the tomatoes with the stock and almond butter until very smooth. Season with salt, pepper and chilli flakes.

3   Wash, trim and quarter the courgette lengthways and then cut into pieces. Halve the peppers, removing seeds and ribs, then wash and dice. Peel and finely dice the garlic. Wash the thyme and pluck and finely chop the leaves. Cook the pasta in boiling salted water according to instructions on the packet. Drain.

4   Heat 3 tablespoons of oil in a non-stick frying pan. Sauté the courgette together with half of the garlic and thyme, stirring constantly, until light golden. Season with salt and pepper and transfer to a container. Put a little more oil in the pan and heat again. Sauté the peppers with the remaining garlic and thyme, stirring constantly for 8–10 minutes. Remove from the heat.

5   Fill bowls with the pasta and add the peppers, courgette and almond sauce. Next, add mozzarella pieces and top with tomato salsa. Garnish with olives and caperberries.

AUTUMN BOWL

INGREDIENTS

FOR THE LENTILS

50 g leek

2 tbsp olive oil

1 tbsp tomato purée

120 g Puy lentils

260 ml vegetable stock

4 sprigs thyme

1 tbsp olive oil

1–2 tsp balsamic vinegar

FOR THE SQUASH

400 g red kuri squash

3 sprigs thyme

½ clove garlic

1 tbsp olive oil

EXTRAS

Roasted beetroot
  (see p. 46) or see tip

1 large handful rocket

100 g feta

Salt and pepper

HERE'S WHAT TO DO

1 Prepare the beetroot as shown on page 46.

2 In the meantime, prepare the lentils. Clean and wash the leek. Cut it along its length into thin strips and then into very small pieces. Heat the olive oil in a pan and sauté the leek until golden. Add the tomato purée and lentils and stir in briefly, then deglaze the pan with the stock. Wash the thyme and add it to the pan. Bring the lentils to the boil then reduce to a simmer and cook for 30–40 minutes. Towards the end, season with the vinegar and salt and pepper.

3 Wash the squash, remove the seeds and fibres and cut the flesh into thin wedges. Wash and shake dry the thyme and pluck and finely chop the leaves. Peel and finely chop the garlic. Mix the thyme and garlic with the olive oil and brush the squash wedges with the mixture. Season with salt and pepper. Add the squash to the baking tray with the beetroot and cook together for the last 20 minutes.

4 Wash and spin dry the rocket. Coarsely crumble the cheese. Take the beetroot and squash out of the oven and leave to cool a little. Fill bowls with the lentils, top with the vegetables, rocket and cheese, and serve.

 SUBSTITUTING

If you prefer, you can also simply peel, thinly slice and dress the beetroot with 2 tablespoons of olive oil, salt and pepper and have it as a raw topping. The pickled beetroot (see p. 47) also makes a great accompaniment.

VEGETARIAN

BEETROOT

WITH COCONUT

INGREDIENTS

2 tbsp desiccated coconut

2 small beetroot (about 180 g)

1 shallot

1 tbsp coconut oil

¼ tsp ground cumin

Salt and pepper

Chilli flakes

HERE'S WHAT TO DO

1 Pour 5 tablespoons of boiling hot water over the coconut and leave to soak for a little while. Peel and coarsely grate the beetroot (do this with care as beetroot stains). Peel and finely dice the shallot.

2 Heat the coconut oil in a frying pan, add the shallot and cumin and sauté until golden. Add the beetroot and sauté for 2–3 minutes. Season with salt, pepper and chilli flakes. Add the coconut and soaking water and cook, covered, for 7–8 minutes. The liquid should evaporate completely.

 TIP

If you prefer, use 2–3 tablespoons of grated fresh coconut instead of dessicated coconut (there's no need to soak it) for a more intense flavour.

ROASTED

INGREDIENTS

3 mixed beetroot (1 red, 1 yellow, 1 Chioggia) (about 100 g each)

4 sprigs thyme

½ clove garlic

1 tbsp olive oil

Salt and pepper

HERE'S WHAT TO DO

1 Heat the oven to 200°C (180°C fan). Peel the beetroot (wear rubber gloves) and then cut each one into 6 wedges. Wash and shake dry the thyme and pluck and coarsely chop the leaves. Peel and slice the garlic.

2 Mix everything with the olive oil, season with salt and pepper and place on a sheet of baking parchment. Fold the parchment into a parcel and close as securely as possible. Place the parcel on a baking tray and roast in the oven (middle shelf) for 35–45 minutes.

QUICK PICKLED

INGREDIENTS

1 shallot

100 ml red wine vinegar

2 ½ tbsp sugar

½ tsp coriander seeds

2 sprigs thyme

2 beetroot (about 120 g)

Salt and pepper

1 tbsp olive oil

HERE'S WHAT TO DO

1 Peel and thinly slice the shallot. Mix the vinegar with 4 tablespoons of water, the sugar and coriander seeds in a saucepan and bring to the boil. Add the thyme and shallot, reduce to a simmer and cook, covered, for 10 minutes.

2 In the meantime, peel the beetroot with a vegetable peeler. Then clean and slice them as thinly as possible (wear rubber gloves; beetroot stains).

3 Season the pickling liquid with salt and pepper, add half of the beetroot and steep for 1–2 minutes over a low heat. Take them out and leave to drain. Add the remaining beetroot and steep for 2 minutes. Next, return the first batch of beetroot to the pan, remove from the heat and cover with a lid. Leave to cool for 1–2 hours.

4 Drain the cooled beetroot well and season with a little salt and pepper. Mix with the olive oil before serving.

VEGAN

WINTER BOWL

INGREDIENTS

FOR THE BRAISED VEGETABLES

1 carrot

1 parsnip (about 100 g)

2 small beetroot

200 g leek

1 red onion

1 clove garlic

1 sprig rosemary

1 organic orange

2 tbsp olive oil

3 pinches chilli flakes

125 ml vegetable stock

FOR THE TOPPING

125 g smoked tofu

Kale with orange (see p. 101)
or see tip

EXTRAS

250 ml vegetable stock

125 g millet

Salt and pepper

HERE'S WHAT TO DO

1 Heat the oven to 190°C (175°C fan). Wash and trim all the vegetables. Peel the carrot and parsnip. Cut the carrot on a diagonal into 3-mm-thick slices, the parsnip into 1-cm-thick batons and the beetroot into eight wedges. Slice the leek into 2-cm-thick rings. Peel the onion and garlic. Cut the onion lengthways into eight wedges and thinly slice the garlic. Wash and shake dry the rosemary and pluck and chop the leaves. Wash the orange in hot water and wipe dry. Grate the zest of one half and squeeze the juice. Put the vegetables into a roasting tin and sprinkle with the rosemary and orange zest.

2 Mix the orange juice with the olive oil and chilli flakes and add to the vegetables. Mix thoroughly and season with salt and pepper. Cook in the oven (middle shelf) for 35–45 minutes, adding the stock after 15 minutes and mixing once or twice with a spoon.

3 In the meantime, prepare the millet. Bring the vegetable stock to the boil in a pan and add the millet. Season lightly with salt if necessary and simmer, covered, over a low heat for 25-30 minutes, or turn off the heat towards the end and leave the grains to swell. Cut the tofu into very thin slices.

4 Fill bowls with millet and serve topped with braised vegetables, kale with orange and tofu.

 SUBSTITUTING

If you prefer, you can also just tear the kale into small pieces and use your hands to rub it with 3 tablespoons of orange juice and a little salt. Then marinate for 30 minutes. Season with salt and pepper.

SPINACH AND HUMMUS BOWL

INGREDIENTS

FOR THE COURGETTES

2 small courgettes

3 tbsp olive oil

FOR THE SPINACH

300 g spinach

1 tbsp olive oil

1 tbsp pine nuts

1 tbsp dried barberries (substitute with dried sour cherries)

FOR THE TOPPING

1 organic baby cucumber

2 tomatoes

1 red pointed pepper

100 g feta cheese

Hummus (see p. 52)

EXTRAS

160 g bulgur

Salt and pepper

½ lemon

HERE'S WHAT TO DO

1 Cook the bulgur according to the instructions on the packet, leave to swell and keep warm if necessary. In the meantime, wash and trim the courgettes and cut lengthways into about 4-mm-thick slices.
Put the courgette slices into a sieve, sprinkle with salt and drain off the water released.

2 Wash and slice the cucumber and the tomatoes. Wash the pepper, remove the seeds and ribs and slice into rings. Cut the lemon into wedges and cut the cheese into cubes.

3 Wash the spinach. Combine the olive oil with the pine nuts in a pan and place over the heat, stirring constantly until the pine nuts turn a light golden colour. Transfer to a container. Put the berries and wet spinach into the pan over a medium heat and wilt them together. Season with salt and pepper and stir in the pine nuts. Remove from the heat, cover with a lid and keep warm.

4 Pat the courgette slices dry with kitchen paper, brush with the olive oil and season with pepper. Heat a griddle pan over a high heat and sear the courgette slices in batches for 2–4 minutes on each side.

5 Fill bowls with bulgur and add the cucumber, tomato, pepper, and cheese. Arrange the spinach, some hummus and griddled courgette slices on one side. Add lemon wedges, for drizzling.

VEGETARIAN

CHICKPEAS

HUMMUS

INGREDIENTS

400 g tin chickpeas

1 clove garlic

1 ½ tbsp tahini (sesame seed paste)

Juice of ½ lemon

3–4 tbsp olive oil

¾ tsp ground cumin

3 pinches each chilli powder and ground turmeric

Salt and pepper

HERE'S WHAT TO DO

Empty the tin of chickpeas into a sieve and collect the liquid. Peel and finely chop the garlic. Combine the chickpeas with the tahini, lemon juice and oil in a mixing beaker and blend with a hand-held blender until smooth, adding chickpea water until the mixture reaches the desired consistency. Season with the spices, salt and pepper.

ROASTED

INGREDIENTS

400 g tin chickpeas

1 clove garlic

2 tbsp olive oil

1 tsp ground cumin

½ tsp ground coriander

¼ tsp ground turmeric

3–4 pinches chilli powder

Salt

HERE'S WHAT TO DO

1 Heat the oven to 200°C (180°C fan). Drain the chickpeas in a sieve, rinse under cold water and leave to drain. Peel and press the garlic through a garlic press into a bowl with the oil. Stir in the spices and season with salt.

2 Add the chickpeas, mix well with the seasoning oil and spread them out on a baking tray lined with baking parchment. Roast the chickpeas in the oven (middle shelf) for 30–40 minutes until crunchy, stirring several times.

 TIP

Depending on the dish you're making, you can roast the chickpeas for 20–25 minutes until the seasoning mixture and outer layer dry out, leaving the chickpeas nice and tender on the inside.

QUICK
CHANA DAL

INGREDIENTS

1 small onion

1 clove garlic

1 piece ginger (10 g)

2 tbsp coconut or
  sunflower oil

1 tomato

1 tsp Indian curry paste
  (shop-bought)

1 tsp tomato purée

400 g tin chickpeas

Salt and pepper

½ tsp garam masala

2 tbsp chopped coriander

HERE'S WHAT TO DO

1 Peel and dice the onion, garlic and ginger. Heat the coconut oil in a pan and slowly sauté the onion over a low heat until golden and soft. In the meantime, wash and remove the stem from the tomato and cut into small dice.

2 Add the garlic and ginger to the onion and cook together for a few moments. Stir in the curry paste and tomato purée. Add the tomato and cook, stirring constantly until all the liquid has evaporated. Empty the chickpeas and liquid from the tin into the pan, season with salt and pepper and cook, covered, over a medium heat for 10 minutes. If necessary, remove the lid and cook for 5 more minutes to evaporate any excess liquid.

3 Stir in the garam masala, season again with salt and pepper and stir in the coriander, setting a little aside to sprinkle over the top.

VEGAN

SUPER QUICK
MILLET BOWL

INGREDIENTS

FOR THE CASHEW CREAM
100 g cashew nuts

1 small onion

3 sprigs thyme

1 tbsp olive oil

½ tsp ground cumin

½ tsp yeast flakes (optional)

FOR THE MILLET
250 ml vegetable stock

125 g millet

FOR THE VEGETABLES
2 small carrots

1 kohlrabi

1 small romanesco cauli-
flower (about 300 g)

EXTRAS
400 g tin chickpeas

Salt and pepper

HERE'S WHAT TO DO

1   For the cashew cream, soak the cashews in cold water for at least 4 hours (or overnight). Drain in a sieve and rinse under cold water. Peel and finely dice the onion. Wash and shake dry the thyme and pluck and finely chop the leaves. Heat the oil in a frying pan and fry the onion over a low heat until golden brown. At the end stir in thyme and cook for a short time. Add the onion mixture to the cashew nuts and blend together with 5–7 tablespoons of water (depending on the desired consistency). Season with salt, pepper, cumin and, optionally, with yeast flakes.

2   For the millet, bring the vegetable stock to the boil in a pan and add the millet. Season lightly with salt if necessary and simmer, covered, over a low heat for 25–30 minutes, or turn off the heat towards the end and leave the grains to swell.

3   In the meantime, wash and trim the vegetables. Peel the carrots and kohlrabi. Break the romanesco into florets, slice the carrots and cut the kohlrabi into batons. Place the individual vegetables side by side in a steamer basket and steam them over a pan filled with a little water for about 20 minutes, seasoning with salt after about 5 minutes.

4   Empty the chickpeas into a sieve, rinse under cold water and leave to drain. Fill bowls with millet and top with the chickpeas and steamed vegetables. Add the cashew cream.

OTSU BOWL

INGREDIENTS

FOR THE SAUCE

½ organic lime

1 piece ginger (10 g)

3 tbsp rice vinegar or white wine vinegar

4 tbsp soy sauce or tamari

½ tsp maple syrup

2 tbsp toasted sesame oil

2–3 pinches chilli flakes

FOR THE TOPPING

1 organic baby cucumber

6 cos lettuce leaves

⅓ bunch coriander

2 spring onions

2 tbsp sesame seeds

EXTRAS

Baked tofu (see p. 111)

150 g soba noodles

Salt

HERE'S WHAT TO DO

1 Make the baked tofu as shown on page 111. In the meantime, make the sauce. Wash the lime in hot water and wipe dry. Grate the zest and squeeze the juice. Peel and grate or finely chop the ginger. Mix the lime zest and ginger well with the remaining ingredients and leave to stand. For more intense sourness, add 3–4 tablespoons of lime juice and salt.

2 Cook the soba noodles according to instructions on the packet. Drain the cooked noodles in a sieve, refresh under cold water and leave to drain thoroughly. Wash and quarter the cucumber lengthways and cut it into small pieces. Wash, shake dry and cut the lettuce leaves crossways into strips. Wash and shake dry the coriander and pluck and coarsely chop the leaves. Clean and trim the spring onions. Slice both white and green parts into thin rings.

3 In a salad bowl, mix the noodles with the cucumber, lettuce, coriander and spring onions (set aside a little of both) with the sauce. Top the noodles with tofu and sprinkle with spring onion, coriander and sesame seeds. Mix everything well before eating.

 TIP

This is a Japanese-style noodle salad. The gluten-free buckwheat noodles, light tofu, refreshing cucumber and lots of herbs make it an ideal summer meal!

VEGAN

VEGETARIAN

KOREAN RICE BOWL

INGREDIENTS

FOR THE OMELETTE

2 spring onions

4 eggs

1 tsp vegetable stock powder

1 tbsp soy sauce or tamari

3 tbsp sunflower oil

2 sheets nori seaweed

FOR THE SPINACH

300 g spinach

1 clove garlic

1 tbsp sesame seeds

1 tsp sunflower oil

1–2 tsp toasted sesame oil

FOR THE TOPPING

1 thick carrot

200 g daikon radish

2 spring onions

EXTRAS

150 g sushi rice (see p. 79)

Salt and pepper

Chilli flakes, for sprinkling

HERE'S WHAT TO DO

1 Prepare the sushi rice as shown on page 79. In the meantime, peel the carrot and radish. Shave ribbons from the carrot with the vegetable peeler and cut the radish into thin batons. Trim and wash the spring onions and cut into thin strips.

2 Wash, sort and leave the spinach to drain. Peel and finely chop the garlic. Toast the sesame seeds in a pan without oil until they release their aroma and then take them out. Put the oil into the pan and sauté the garlic. Add the wet spinach, season with salt and pepper, and wilt the leaves over a high heat. Drain the spinach in a sieve, squeezing a little if necessary, and mix with the sesame oil.

3 For the omelette, wash and trim the spring onions, keeping both white and green parts, and cut lengthways into thin strips. Then dice them as finely as possible. Mix them with the eggs, vegetable stock powder, 2 tablespoons of water and the soy sauce in a bowl and lightly season with salt and pepper. Heat half the oil in a frying pan and then add half the egg mixture. Cook over a low heat until lightly set but still moist. Place a nori sheet on top, press lightly and, starting from one end, roll up the omelette, pressing well throughout the process. Transfer to a plate and cook a second omelette in the same way with the rest of the egg mixture. Leave the rolls to cool a little and cut into slices.

4 Fill bowls with rice. Arrange omelette slices on top. Add the spinach, sprinkle with sesame seeds and arrange radish batons and carrot ribbons to one side. Finish by adding strips of spring onion and sprinkle with chilli flakes if desired.

 SUBSTITUTING

If you prefer, you can swap the raw radish and carrots for Japanese-style pickles (see p. 40).

VEGAN

INDIAN DAL BOWL

INGREDIENTS

FOR THE DAL

1 onion

1 piece ginger (10 g)

2 tomatoes

1 tbsp coconut oil

⅓ tsp cumin seeds

1 tsp curry powder

100 g red lentils

150 ml coconut milk

150 ml vegetable stock

1–2 dash(es) lime juice

FOR THE CAULIFLOWER

1 small cauliflower (about 400 g)

Coconut oil, for frying

½ tsp cumin

1 ½ tsp ground coriander

1 tsp ground cumin

½ tsp ground turmeric

¼ tsp chilli powder

EXTRAS

150 g rice (preferably basmati)

1 handful baby spinach

1 tbsp chopped coriander (optional)

Salt

HERE'S WHAT TO DO

1 For the dal, peel and finely dice the onion and ginger. Wash and remove the stem from the tomatoes and cut into small dice. Heat the coconut oil in a pan and sauté the onion, ginger, tomatoes and cumin seeds over a medium heat until the onion turns a light golden colour. Add the curry powder and lentils, cook briefly and then pour in the coconut milk and vegetable stock. Cover with a lid and cook over medium heat for 20–25 minutes.

2 In the meantime, cook the rice according to the instructions on the packet. Wash, trim and cut the cauliflower into florets. Cut the florets into slightly smaller pieces and put them into a steamer basket and season with salt. Steam the cauliflower over a pan filled with a little water for 10–15 minutes; it should stay quite firm.

3 Wash, sort and spin dry the spinach. Transfer the cauliflower to a container and leave to cool a little. Heat plenty of coconut oil in a pan and toast the cumin. Add the cauliflower and remaining spices, season with salt and fry the cauliflower until nicely golden.

4 Fill bowls with rice and top with the spinach, spiced and fried cauliflower and dal. Optionally, sprinkle with chopped coriander.

ALADDIN'S WONDERFUL BOWL

INGREDIENTS

FOR THE TAHINI SAUCE

1 small clove garlic

2 tbsp tahini (sesame seed paste)

3 tbsp yoghurt (3.5% fat)

3–4 tbsp lemon juice

FOR THE TABBOULEH

80 g parsley

1 large tomato

2 spring onions

1–2 tbsp lemon juice

2 tbsp olive oil

EXTRAS

160 g bulgur

250 g broccoli

Easy falafel (see p. 65) or see tip

Salt and pepper

HERE'S WHAT TO DO

1   Make the falafel as shown on page 65. In the meantime, cook the bulgur according to the instructions on the packet and leave to swell. Wash and trim the broccoli and cut it into small florets. Peel the stalk and cut it into pieces. Put both florets and stalk pieces in a steamer basket and steam over a pan filled with a little water over a medium heat for 20–25 minutes. Season with salt after steaming for a short time.

2   For the tahini sauce, peel and press the garlic through a garlic press. Mix the garlic with the tahini and yoghurt until smooth and then add the lemon juice and, depending on the desired consistency, 5–7 tablespoons of water. Finally, season with salt and pepper.

3   For the tabbouleh, wash the parsley, pluck and spin dry the leaves and tear or cut them into small pieces. Wash, dry and halve the tomato. Scoop out the seeds with a spoon and cut the flesh into small dice. Clean and trim the spring onions. Slice both white and green parts into rings. Whisk the lemon juice with the olive oil, season with salt and pepper and mix with the other ingredients.

4   Fill bowls with the bulgur and top with broccoli, tabbouleh and a few falafel. Put a dollop of sauce in the middle or spread a little over the broccoli and falafel.

 TIP

If you're in a hurry, instead of making falafel, simply drain chickpeas from a tin and add them to the bowl.

VEGETARIAN

VEGAN

EASY FALAFEL

INGREDIENTS

400 g tin chickpeas

1 tbsp ground linseed

1 small onion

1 clove garlic

2 tbsp olive oil

3–4 sprigs each coriander
  and parsley

1 ½ tsp ground cumin

2 pinches chilli powder

Juice of ½ lemon

1 tbsp tahini (sesame seed
  paste)

Salt and pepper

HERE'S WHAT TO DO

1 Heat the oven to 220°C (200°C fan) and line a baking tray with baking parchment. Empty the tin of chickpeas into a sieve, collecting the liquid, and leave to drain. Whisk the ground linseed with 6–8 tablespoons of water until smooth and leave to swell for 15 minutes.

2 Peel and coarsely chop the onion and garlic. Heat 1 tablespoon of olive oil in a small nonstick frying pan and sauté the onion and garlic until golden. Remove from the heat and leave to cool slightly.

3 In the meantime, wash the coriander and parsley, pat dry well with kitchen paper and coarsely chop together with the stems. Blend the chickpeas, onion and garlic mixture, spices, lemon juice and tahini to a coarse paste in a food processor. If the paste is too dry, dilute with a little of the chickpea liquid.

4 Stir in the linseed paste until smooth and season the mixture with salt and pepper. Shape the mixture into 12 balls and lightly flatten into discs. Place them on the baking tray and brush them all over with oil. Bake the falafel in the oven (middle shelf) for 25–30 minutes, turning them over once or twice.

GADO GADO BOWL

 VEGAN

INGREDIENTS

FOR THE CABBAGE SALAD

300 g pointed cabbage

Sugar

1 tbsp lime juice

FOR THE PEANUT SAUCE

1 shallot

1 clove garlic

1 tbsp sunflower oil

1 small tin coconut milk (160 ml)

1 ½ tbsp peanut butter

3 tbsp soy sauce or tamari

½ tsp demerara sugar

½–1 tsp chilli sauce (e.g. sriracha)

2–3 tbsp lime juice

FOR THE VEGETABLES

1 red pointed pepper

1 carrot

2 sticks celery

1 clove garlic

2 tbsp sunflower oil

2 tbsp soy sauce or tamari

1 tbsp lime juice

EXTRAS

150 g flat rice noodles (e.g. pad Thai noodles)

200 g tempeh

Oil, for frying

2 tbsp chopped coriander

Salt

HERE'S WHAT TO DO

1 For the cabbage salad, wash and quarter the cabbage and completely cut out the hard stem. Use a knife or a mandoline to cut the quarters crossways into very fine strips. Add a generous pinch of salt and sugar and the lime juice to the cabbage and knead it with your hands until nice and soft. Then leave to marinate.

2 For the sauce, peel and finely chop the shallot and garlic. Sauté in a pan with the oil over a low heat until translucent and then deglaze the pan with the coconut milk and 5 tablespoons of water. Simmer for 5 minutes, uncovered, and then stir in the remaining ingredients, setting aside 1 tablespoon of lime juice. Simmer the sauce, uncovered, for 10 more minutes, stirring occasionally. Season to taste with the remaining lime juice.

3 Heat the oven to 150°C (fan not recommended). Cook the noodles according to the instructions on the packet. Cut the tempeh into 1-cm-thick slices. Heat plenty of oil in a frying pan and fry the tempeh on both sides over a medium heat until golden brown. Drain on kitchen paper and pat dry, then place the slices on a baking tray lined with baking parchment and finish cooking them in the oven (middle shelf) for 10 minutes.

4 In the meantime, quarter, trim, wash and cut the peppers crossways into strips. Peel and quarter the carrot lengthways and then cut it on a diagonal into thin slices. Wash and clean the celery and cut it on a diagonal into thin strips. Peel and finely chop the garlic. Heat oil in a wok and stir-fry vegetables and garlic over a high heat. Deglaze the wok with the soy sauce and lime juice, continue to stir-fry for a short time and then remove from the heat.

5 Drain the noodles well and divide them into bowls. Top with the vegetables, cabbage, tempeh and peanut sauce. Optionally, sprinkle with chopped coriander. Mix everything together before eating.

BAVARIAN BOWL

INGREDIENTS

FOR THE CREAM CHEESE DIP

1 shallot

80 g ripe camembert cheese

80 g double cream cheese

1 tsp white wine vinegar

Salt and pepper

3 pinches ground caraway seeds

¾ tsp sweet paprika

FOR THE RADISH MIX

1 tbsp pumpkin seeds

6 radishes

1 punnet growing cress (e.g. watercress)

EXTRAS

125 g durum wheat (Ebly®)

1 small bunch chives

120 g sauerkraut

2 tbsp clarified butter

HERE'S WHAT TO DO

1 For the cream cheese dip, peel and finely dice the shallot. Cut the camembert into small cubes and using a fork, mix it with the shallot, cream cheese and vinegar. Season with the ground caraway seeds, paprika and a generous amount of salt and pepper.

2 Prepare the radish mix. Toast pumpkin seeds in a dry frying pan until they release their aroma. Leave to cool. Wash, trim and slice the radishes. Wash the cress and snip the stems from the bed. Coarsely chop the pumpkin seeds and mix them with radishes and cress.

3 Prepare the durum wheat according to the instructions on the packet. Wash and chop the chives. Tear the sauerkraut into small pieces and pat dry well with kitchen paper. Melt the clarified butter in a non-stick frying pan. Sauté the sauerkraut over a medium to high heat until it darkens and begins to turn brown, then season with salt and pepper.

4 Mix some of the chives into the cream cheese mixture. Fill bowls with durum wheat. Top with the sauerkraut and radish mix and add a dollop of cream cheese dip to one side. Sprinkle with chives.

VEGETARIAN

VEGETARIAN

MUHAMMARA BOWL

INGREDIENTS

FOR THE MUHAMMARA

2 red peppers

1 clove garlic

3 tbsp olive oil

6 tbsp orange juice

1 slice toasting bread

30 g shelled walnuts

1–2 tbsp red wine vinegar

2–3 pinches chilli flakes

¾ tsp ground cumin

FOR THE CABBAGE

1 small pointed cabbage

2 tbsp olive oil

EXTRAS

125 g couscous

6 large Lollo Rosso lettuce leaves

6 labneh balls (see p. 72)

1 tsp nigella seeds

Salt and pepper

HERE'S WHAT TO DO

1 For the muhammara, halve, trim, wash and cut the peppers into small pieces. Peel and chop the garlic. Heat the oil in a frying pan and sauté the peppers over a high heat for about 3 minutes, stirring constantly. Season with salt. Add the garlic and sauté for a short time. Deglaze the pan with the orange juice and cook over a medium heat for 6–7 minutes until the peppers are soft and the liquid has almost completely reduced. Add water if necessary. Leave to cool. Toast the bread, toast the walnuts in a dry frying pan and leave both to cool and coarsely chop them. Combine with the cooled pepper pieces and vinegar and blend until very smooth with a hand blender. Season with salt, chilli flakes and cumin.

2 In the meantime, quarter the cabbage. Heat the oil in a non-stick frying pan and sauté the cabbage quarters over a medium heat until light golden all over. Season with salt and pepper. Add 100 ml of water and simmer, covered, for 6–8 minutes.

3 Cook the couscous according to the instructions on the packet. Wash and spin dry the lettuce leaves and tear to make a little smaller. Pat dry the labneh balls with kitchen paper.

4 Fill two bowls with couscous and place two cabbage quarters in each. Arrange lettuce leaves next to them and top with the labneh balls. Add a dollop of muhammara in the middle and sprinkle nigella seeds over the labneh balls and cabbage.

LABNEH BALLS

INGREDIENTS

1 kg Greek yoghurt
   (10% fat)

Salt

500 ml olive oil

3 sprigs thyme

2 small dried chilli peppers

½ tsp peppercorns

1 tsp nigella seeds

HERE'S WHAT TO DO

1 Line a fine-mesh sieve with clean muslin, allowing a good length of cloth to hang over the sides. Lightly salt the yoghurt and pour it into the muslin. Bring the corners of the cloth together and twist closed. Tie it with a piece of string to make a small pouch. Attach the pouch to the handle of a spoon and hang it over a large bowl. Leave the yoghurt to drain in the refrigerator for 1–3 days until it turns dry and slightly crumbly.

2 With oiled hands, shape the yoghurt into small balls (about 3 cm in diameter). In a clean clip-top storage jar, arrange the balls in layers with thyme, chilli peppers and peppercorns between the layers. Add the nigella seeds and pour in olive oil to cover well.

3 Seal the jar and refrigerate. Marinate for at least 2–3 days. They will keep for up to 3 weeks.

 TIP

If you can't wait that long, use the freshly made balls without marinating them. You can sprinkle them with fresh chopped herbs, spice mixtures (e.g. dukkah, see p. 32) or simply chilli flakes or nigella seeds. Season them with salt and pepper and drizzle with olive oil. They're perfect not just for bowls, but with bread, salad or on their own as an appetiser.

VEGETARIAN

CHILLI SIN CARNE BOWL

VEGETARIAN

INGREDIENTS

FOR THE TOMATO SALSA

2 tomatoes

1 small red onion

2 tbsp chopped coriander

Demerara sugar

1–2 tsp lime juice

1 tbsp olive oil

FOR THE CHILLI

400 g tin kidney beans

1 small onion

1 clove garlic

1 tbsp olive oil

1 tbsp tomato purée

1 tsp chilli con carne seasoning mix (shop-bought)

FOR THE TOPPING

1 avocado (see tip)

1 tsp lime juice

½ head cos lettuce

1 spring onion

3 tbsp sour cream

EXTRAS

120 g rice (preferably long-grain)

Salt and pepper

HERE'S WHAT TO DO

1   For the salsa, halve the tomatoes, deseed with a teaspoon and finely dice the flesh. Peel and roughly dice the onion. Combine and season with coriander, salt, pepper, a good pinch of sugar and the lime juice. Mix with the oil and leave to marinate.

2   Cook the rice according to the instructions on the packet. In the meantime, empty the tin of beans into a sieve and collect the liquid. Peel and finely chop the onion and garlic. Heat the oil in a small frying pan and sauté the onion and garlic until golden. Stir in the tomato purée, cook together for a short time and then add the beans and some of the liquid from the tin. Season with the chilli con carne mix. Cook, uncovered, for 5 minutes over medium heat. Add more of the liquid if necessary; the final consistency should be thick and creamy. Season with salt.

3   In the meantime halve, stone and peel the avocado. Slice the flesh lengthways and drizzle it immediately with lime juice. Lightly season with salt and pepper. Wash, spin dry and cut the lettuce into strips. Clean and trim the spring onions. Slice both white and green parts into thin rings. Stir the sour cream until smooth and season with salt and pepper.

4   Fill bowls with rice. Cover one side with the chilli, and arrange lettuce strips, salsa and avocado slices next to it. Put a dollop of sour cream on the side and sprinkle over everything with spring onion.

 TIP

Guacamole (see p. 83) makes a good alternative to the avocado slices for this bowl.

RICE NOODLES WITH PRAWNS

INGREDIENTS

FOR THE SEASONING SAUCE

1 piece ginger (10 g)

Juice of 1 lime

1 tsp demerara sugar

2 tbsp fish sauce

EXTRAS

1 organic baby cucumber

1 red pointed pepper

1 thick carrot

½ head cos lettuce

½ bunch coriander

180 g Vietnamese rice vermicelli noodles

200 g frozen tiger prawns (ready to cook, unpeeled)

1 small clove garlic

2 sticks lemongrass

2 tbsp peanut oil

½ tsp chilli sauce (e.g. sriracha)

HERE'S WHAT TO DO

1 For the sauce, peel and dice the ginger as finely as possible. Mix well with the lime juice, sugar, fish sauce and 6 tablespoons of water.

2 Wash, halve lengthways and cut the cucumber into pieces. Quarter the peppers lengthways. Trim, wash and cut them crossways into thin strips. Peel and trim the carrot. Use a knife or mandoline to slice it into thin batons. Wash, trim and spin dry the lettuce. Then cut it crossways into thin strips. Wash and shake dry the coriander and pluck and coarsely chop the leaves.

3 Cook the noodles in water according to the instructions on the packet and drain in a sieve. Rinse the prawns under cold water and pat dry well. Peel and finely chop the garlic. Trim off the base and top of the lemon grass, cut the bottom 8–10-cm section lengthways into thin strips and then chop very finely.

4 Heat the oil in a wok over a high heat. Add the prawns, garlic and lemongrass and stir-fry until the prawns turn pink. Lower the heat, add the chilli sauce and 125 ml of water and cook over a medium-high heat until the liquid has evaporated. Add the noodles, vegetables and seasoning sauce. Mix everything together and heat through. Remove from the heat, mix in the lettuce and coriander and serve immediately in bowls.

FISH

FISH

SUSHI BOWL

INGREDIENTS

FOR THE SUSHI RICE

150 g sushi rice

2 tbsp rice vinegar

1 tbsp sugar

FOR THE SEAWEED

2 tbsp dried wakame sea-
weed (preferably organic)

1 tsp sesame seeds

1 tsp toasted sesame oil

1 tsp lime juice

Sugar

FOR THE TOPPING

180 g frozen shelled eda-
mame beans

180 g very fresh salmon fillet (skinless)

1 thick carrot

1 organic baby cucumber

EXTRAS

Salt and pepper

Shichimi togarashi (see tip)

HERE'S WHAT TO DO

1   Cook the rice according to the instructions on the packet. In the meantime, combine the vinegar, sugar and half
a teaspoon of salt in a small saucepan and heat while stirring until the sugar is completely dissolved. Leave to cool.
Cover the freshly cooked rice in the pot with a tea towel
and leave to cool for 15 minutes. Transfer to a wide bowl
and spread out flat. Sprinkle the vinegar mixture over the
rice and use a spoon handle to carefully fold it into the
rice. Leave it to cool completely.

2   In the meantime, wash the seaweed in a sieve under cold
water. Soak in cold water for 15 minutes and drain in a
sieve. Cook in water for 4–5 minutes according to the instructions on the packet. Drain and refresh under cold
water and then leave to drain. Toast the sesame seeds in
a dry frying pan and leave to cool. Mix the sesame oil
with the lime juice, add seaweed and sesame seeds, and
season with a little salt, pepper and a pinch of sugar.

3   Heat salted water in a pan and cook the frozen edamame, covered, for 10 minutes over a medium heat. Drain in
a sieve, refresh under cold water and then leave to drain.
Meanwhile, rinse the salmon under cold water, pat dry
with kitchen paper and thinly slice. Peel and cut the carrot into thin sticks. Wash and cut the cucumber into thin
sticks, removing the seeds if necessary.

4   Fill bowls with rice and arrange the seaweed, edamame,
carrot, cucumber and salmon on the top. Sprinkle with
shichimi togarashi as desired.

 TIP

Shichimi togarashi is a blend of seven spices and peppers, including mild sansho pepper and hot chilli flakes. It can be
found at Oriental food shops.

HOT TUNA BOWL

INGREDIENTS

FOR THE TUNA TARTARE

1 tbsp sesame seeds

180 g very fresh tuna fillet

1 tbsp toasted sesame oil

2 tbsp chilli sauce (e.g. sriracha)

1 spring onion

FOR THE SEAWEED AND SESAME SEED SPRINKLES

1 tbsp each black and white sesame seeds

½ tsp fleur de sel

2 pinches chilli flakes

1 ½ tbsp roasted nori flakes

EXTRAS

150 g sushi rice (see p. 79)

Marinated avocado (see p. 82)

150 g mangetout

Salt

8 radishes

HERE'S WHAT TO DO

1   Prepare the sushi rice as shown on page 79. For the tuna tartare, toast the sesame seeds in a dry frying pan and leave to cool. In the meantime, rinse the tuna under cold water and pat dry with kitchen paper. Using a knife, cut the tuna into small dice and then chop very finely. Mix it with the sesame oil and chilli sauce. Wash and dry the spring onion. Slice the green part into very thin rings and mix into the tartare together with the sesame seeds. Slice the white part into thin rings as well.

2   Make the marinated avocado as shown on page 82. Wash, trim and slice the mangetout on a diagonal into thin strips. Bring salted water to the boil and cook the mangetout for barely 1 minute. Then drain in a sieve, refresh under cold water and leave to drain. Trim, wash and thinly slice the radishes.

3   For the sprinkles, toast the sesame seeds in a dry frying pan until they release their aroma. Then take them out and leave to cool. Coarsely crush the fleur de sel and chilli flakes in a mortar and then mix in the nori flakes.

4   Fill bowls with rice and top with tuna tartare, avocado, radish and mangetout. Finish with the sprinkles and white onion rings.

FISH

AVOCADO

MAYONNAISE

INGREDIENTS

1 ripe avocado

1 clove garlic

3 tbsp olive oil

2–3 tbsp lemon juice

Salt and pepper

HERE'S WHAT TO DO

Halve and stone the avocado. Scoop out the flesh with a spoon into a mixing bowl or blender. Peel the garlic clove and press through a garlic press over the avocado. Add the olive oil and 2 tablespoons of lemon juice and blend to a smooth cream. Season to taste with salt, pepper and lemon juice.

MARINATED

INGREDIENTS

1 tbsp sesame seeds

1 avocado

1–2 tsp lime juice

1 piece ginger (5 g)

1 spring onion

1 tbsp dry sherry

1 tbsp rice vinegar or
   white wine vinegar

1 tsp maple syrup

Salt

Chilli flakes

HERE'S WHAT TO DO

1 Toast the sesame seeds in a dry frying pan until they turn golden. Halve, stone and peel the avocado. Cut the flesh into small dice. Mix it immediately with 1 teaspoon of lime juice to stop the flesh from turning brown.

2 Peel and very finely chop the ginger. Clean and trim the spring onion. Slice the green part into quite thin rings. Make a marinade by mixing the ginger with the sherry, vinegar and maple syrup. Season with salt and 1–3 pinches of chilli flakes. Mix with the avocado, spring onion and sesame seeds and marinate for 10 minutes. Season to taste with the remaining lime juice.

GUACAMOLE

INGREDIENTS

1 tomato

1 spring onion

1 ripe avocado

2 tbsp lime juice

½ tsp ground cumin

Salt and pepper

HERE'S WHAT TO DO

1   Wash and halve the tomato. Scoop out the seeds with a spoon and cut the flesh into small dice. Trim and wash the spring onion. Cut the white part lengthways into thin strips and finely chop. Slice the green part into thin rings.

2   Halve, stone and peel the avocado. Roughly chop the flesh and drizzle with lime juice. According to preference, crush the flesh more or less coarsely with a fork. Mix in the white part of the spring onion and diced tomato. Season with the cumin and salt and pepper. Add a little more lime juice if necessary. Gently mix in part of the green spring onion rings and sprinkle the rest over the top.

SUPER
BOWLS

VEGAN

COLOURS OF ASIA BOWL

INGREDIENTS

FOR THE RED CABBAGE SALAD

150 g red cabbage

Juice of 1 lime

1 piece ginger (10 g)

½–1 tsp brown sugar

FOR THE CORIANDER CREAM

½ bunch coriander

½ clove garlic

200 g silken tofu

4 tbsp olive oil

2 tbsp lime juice

2 pinches chilli flakes

FOR THE TOPPING

1 carrot

1 yellow pepper

Coriander, for garnishing

EXTRAS

Salt and pepper

Grilled sweet potato (see p. 107)

120 g rice (preferably basmati)

HERE'S WHAT TO DO

1   Wash the cabbage and cut out the hard core as a wedge. Use a knife or mandoline to cut the cabbage into thin strips. Add a generous pinch of salt and 2 tablespoons of lime juice and knead well with your hands until it is nice and soft (wear rubber gloves; the cabbage will stain). Peel and finely dice the ginger. Mix it with the remaining lime juice and the brown sugar until the sugar is dissolved. Season with salt and pepper, mix with the red cabbage and leave to stand.

2   In the meantime, grill the sweet potato on bamboo skewers (see p. 107). Cook the rice according to the instructions on the packet. Peel and coarsely grate the carrot. Halve, trim, wash and cut the pepper into thin strips.

3   For the coriander cream, wash the coriander, shake dry well and pluck the leaves. Peel the garlic clove and press through a garlic press. Combine it with the tofu in a mixing beaker and add the coriander, oil and lime juice. Blend to a smooth cream with a hand blender and season with salt and pepper.

4   Fill bowls with rice and arrange sweet potato skewers, red cabbage salad, grated carrot and pepper strips on top. Put the coriander cream in the centre and sprinkle with chilli flakes. Sprinkle the bowl with coriander and mint leaves.

BIBIMBAP BOWL

VEGETARIAN

INGREDIENTS

FOR THE VEGETABLES

1 thick carrot

6 radishes

100 g king oyster mush-
rooms

100 g baby spinach

2 cloves garlic

3 spring onions

3 tbsp soy sauce or tamari

Chilli flakes

2 tbsp toasted sesame oil

1 tbsp rice vinegar or white
wine vinegar

3 tbsp sunflower oil

FOR THE MISO SAUCE

2 tbsp miso paste

½ tsp chilli sauce (e.g.
sriracha)

1 tbsp toasted sesame oil

EXTRAS

150 g rice (preferably
basmati)

2 eggs

Kimchi (see p. 90)

1½ tbsp black sesame seeds

Sugar

Salt and pepper

HERE'S WHAT TO DO

1 Peel the carrot and use the vegetable peeler to shave it into wide ribbons. Wash, trim and slice the radishes. Clean the mush- rooms. Cut off the stems and slice into 4-mm-thick discs. Slice the caps vertically. Wash and spin dry the baby spinach leaves. Peel the garlic. Wash and shake dry the spring onions and cut the white and green parts separately into thin rings.

2 Mix the carrot with 1 tablespoon of soy sauce, two-thirds of a teaspoon of chilli flakes, a quarter of a garlic clove, half the green spring onion rings, half a tablespoon of sesame oil and a little salt and knead vigorously. Mix the radish slices with the vinegar, a pinch of sugar and a quarter of a garlic clove.

3 Heat 1½ tablespoons of sunflower oil in a frying pan and sau- té the mushrooms with half a clove of garlic, stirring con- stantly, until lightly browned. Then season with salt and pep- per and remove from the heat. Mix in half of the remaining green spring onion rings. Clean the frying pan and heat an- other half a tablespoon sunflower oil. Add the rest of the gar- lic and the spinach and sauté, stirring constantly. Deglaze the pan with 2 tablespoons of soy sauce and, while continuing to stir, add 3 tablespoons of water and cook over a medium heat for 2–3 minutes until the spinach is firm to the bite. Re- move from the heat and stir in half a tablespoon of sesame oil and a little more green spring onion rings. Then leave all the vegetables to steep in their respective liquids – ideally for 1 hour, or until the rice is cooked.

4 Cook the rice according to the instructions on the packet. In the meantime, make the miso sauce. Mix the miso paste with the chilli sauce, 1 tablespoon of sesame oil, 3 tablespoons of water and a pinch of sugar until smooth. Finely chop 1 tea- spoon of white spring onion rings and stir into the sauce.

5 Drain the cooked rice if necessary and keep warm. Heat the remaining sunflower oil in a non-stick frying pan. Fry the eggs, keeping the yolk as runny as possible. Season with salt and pepper.

6 To serve, fill bowls with rice, pour some sauce in the middle of the rice and cover it with a fried egg. Arrange the individu- al vegetables and kimchi side by side around the egg. Sprin- kle over everything with sesame seeds and the remaining spring onion rings.

KIMCHI

INGREDIENTS

300 g Chinese leaf cabbage

150 g sea salt (preferably natural, untreated and un-refined)

2 tbsp dried shrimp (from Oriental food shops)

1 small onion

4 cloves garlic

1 piece ginger (10 g)

1 small apple

2 tbsp rice flour (substitute with 3 tbsp cooked rice)

4 tbsp fish sauce

1 tbsp sugar

About 70 g Korean red chilli flakes (gochugaru, from Oriental food shops)

Salt

HERE'S WHAT TO DO

1 Halve the cabbage lengthways and cut out the woody core. Wash the leaves thoroughly, then cut across into about 4-cm-wide strips. Halve the thicker parts length-ways. Make a brine by dissolving the salt in a little hot water and then top it up with cold water to make 1.5 litres. Put the cabbage into a large bowl and pour the brine over it. Weigh down the cabbage with a board or plate to keep it well covered in brine. Cover the bowl with a cloth and soak for about 12 hours (preferably over-night); the cabbage should soften and become pliable.

2 The next day, make the seasoning paste. Bring 200 ml of water to the boil, add the dried shrimp and simmer, cov-ered, for about 10 minutes. Then leave to cool.

3 Peel and coarsely chop the onion, garlic and ginger. Wash, core, quarter and roughly chop the apple. Com-bine everything with the shrimp and soaking liquid in a food processor and blend until very smooth. Blend in the rice flour or cooked rice. Transfer the mixture to a bowl and add the fish sauce. Gradually stir in as much of the chilli flakes that you consider will make the kimchi pleas-antly spicy.

4 Put the cabbage into a wash basin and rinse well two or three times to get rid of all the salt. The leaves should still taste pleasantly salty. Leave the cabbage to drain well and then mix with the seasoning paste – simply knead well wearing disposable latex gloves. Season again to taste with chilli flakes, salt and sugar or fish sauce if necessary and transfer everything to a large clip-top storage jar.

Pour just under 100 ml of water into the bowl to dissolve any remaining paste. Then pour the water over the cabbage to cover well and remove any trapped air bubbles from the jar. Close loosely with the lid.

5   Leave the kimchi to stand for 2–4 days at room temperature to steep the cabbage well. By this time fermentation will have started. Air bubbles form and rise to the top and the mixture will 'bubble' to a lesser or greater extent. Now close the lid securely and put the jar in the refrigerator. Leave the kimchi to 'ripen' further (it will be necessary to open the lid from time to time to release the gases that form). The kimchi can be eaten right away , but its flavour is at its best after 1–2 months.

 ## TIP FOR VEGETARIANS

Instead of the shrimp, you can use 200 ml of light vegetable stock, and you can substitute the fish sauce with soy sauce. In this case, Korean soup soy sauce (joseon ganjang, from Oriental food shops) is the most suitable.

VEGETARIAN

APHRODITE'S
BEAUTY BOWL

INGREDIENTS

FOR THE PARSLEY PESTO

40 g almonds

1 small bunch parsley

½ clove garlic

½ organic lemon

80–100 ml olive oil

FOR THE PEPPERS

2 red pointed peppers

½ clove garlic

3 sprigs thyme

Juice of 1 orange

FOR THE TOPPING

125 g baby spinach

200 g halloumi cheese

2 tbsp small black olives

EXTRAS

120 g couscous

Olive oil, for frying

Salt and pepper

HERE'S WHAT TO DO

1   For the pesto, coarsely chop the almonds and toast in a dry frying pan until light golden. Leave to cool. In the meantime, wash the parsley and pat dry well with kitchen paper. Pluck and coarsely chop the leaves. Peel and coarsely chop the garlic. Wash the lemon under hot water and dry it. Finely grate the zest and squeeze the juice. Blend the almonds, parsley and half a teaspoon of lemon zest with 2 tablespoons of lemon juice and just over half the olive oil. Then gradually add as much oil as necessary to achieve the desired consistency. Finally, season with salt and pepper.

2   Halve, trim, wash and cut the peppers into small pieces. Peel and slice the garlic. Wash and shake dry the thyme and pluck and finely chop the leaves. Heat 2 tablespoons of oil in a frying pan and sauté the peppers and garlic over a high heat, stirring constantly, until the peppers are lightly browned. Add the thyme, season with salt and pepper and deglaze the pan with half the orange juice. Cook over a medium heat for 5–7 minutes gradually adding the rest of the orange juice. All the liquid should evaporate by the end of this time.

3   Wash, sort and spin dry the spinach. Cook the couscous according to the instructions on the packet. Pat dry the cheese with kitchen paper and cut it crossways into 1-cm-thick slices. Lightly brush a griddle pan with oil and place it over the heat. Fry the cheese until lightly browned on both sides.

4   Fill bowls with couscous and arrange the halloumi and spinach over the top. Drizzle both with pesto. Arrange the peppers and olives to the side.

CHANA DAL BOWL

INGREDIENTS

FOR THE MINT RAITA

½ bunch mint

4 sprigs coriander

150 g Greek yoghurt
(10% fat)

½ tsp ground cumin

Demerara sugar

FOR THE RADISH

1 small daikon radish

2 tbsp sunflower oil

¼ tsp ground turmeric

2 pinches sweet paprika

½ tsp nigella seeds

FOR THE TOPPING

1 organic baby cucumber

Paneer cheese (see p. 97, or
shop-bought)

EXTRAS

150 g rice (preferably basmati)

Quick chana dal (see p. 53)

Salt and pepper

Oil, for frying

HERE'S WHAT TO DO

1 For the raita, wash the mint and coriander. Pluck and coarsely chop the leaves and purée or finely chop them with 1 tablespoon of yoghurt in a food processor. Mix in the remaining yoghurt and the cumin and season with salt, pepper and 2 pinches of demerara sugar. Then leave to stand in the refrigerator.

2 In the meantime, cook the rice according to the instructions on the packet and leave to rest. At the same time, make the chana dal as shown on page 53 and keep warm if necessary. Wash and slice the cucumber.

3 Prepare the radish. Peel and cut the radish into 2-mm-thick slices. Heat the oil in a non-stick frying pan and add the radish, turmeric and paprika. Sprinkle with nigella seeds and stir for a short time. Then cook over a low heat for 10 minutes, covered if possible. Add 1–2 tablespoons of water if necessary.

4 Slice the paneer. Brush a griddle pan with oil and fry the cheese on both sides for 3–4 minutes.

5 Fill bowls with rice, top with the chana dal, radish, cucumber and paneer and add a dollop of mint raita in the middle.

VEGETARIAN

VEGETARIAN

PANEER INDIAN-STYLE FRESH CHEESE

INGREDIENTS

2 litres fresh whole milk

6–8 tbsp freshly squeezed
lemon juice or
wine vinegar

HERE'S WHAT TO DO

1 Slowly heat the milk in a pan, stirring until it comes to the boil. Then add the lemon juice or vinegar. The milk will curdle and separate into a yellowish whey and white flaky curds – this may take some time so you should leave the pan on the heat for as long as it takes. If nothing happens, add some more lemon juice or vinegar. Once the milk has curdled, take the pan off the heat.

2 Pour the contents of the pan into a fine sieve and rinse thoroughly under cold water while stirring with a spoon. Drain well. Line a second sieve with clean muslin or a tea towel. Add the curds. Bring the corners of the cloth together and twist tightly to squeeze out as much liquid as possible.

3 Line a small rectangular mould with the cloth. Fill the mould with the now dry and crumbly curds and press down firmly with your hands. Fold the cloth over the curds, place a cutting board on top and add weights, such as tins of food, and then press down as firmly as possible. Leave in the refrigerator to firm up for 8 hours (or overnight). This cheese tastes good fresh or cut into slices and fried.

TUSCANY BOWL

INGREDIENTS

FOR THE TOMATOES

300 g cherry tomatoes

1 small clove garlic

1 sprig rosemary

1 ½ tbsp olive oil

1 tsp balsamic vinegar

Sugar

FOR THE BEANS

400 g tin haricot beans

½ clove garlic

8 sage leaves

1 tbsp olive oil

1 tsp tomato purée

EXTRAS

125 g durum wheat (Ebly®)

Salt and pepper

Steamed cavolo nero (see p. 100)

HERE'S WHAT TO DO

1 Heat the oven to 200°C (180°C fan). Wash the tomatoes and put them into a small ovenproof dish. Peel and slice the garlic. Wash the rosemary and pluck and finely chop the leaves. Add the garlic to the tomatoes, scatter over the rosemary and drizzle with olive oil and balsamic vinegar. Season with salt and pepper and sprinkle with a pinch of sugar. Cook in the oven (middle shelf) for 20–25 minutes, stirring once after about 15 minutes.

2 In the meantime, cook the durum wheat according to the instructions on the packet and keep warm. Cook the cavolo nero as shown on page 100.

3 At the same time, prepare the beans. Empty the tin of beans into a sieve and collect the liquid. Peel and finely chop the garlic, rub the sage leaves and cut them into strips. Heat the olive oil in a small frying pan and sauté the garlic and sage. Stir in the tomato purée. Add some of the liquid from the tin and the beans. Season with salt and pepper. Cook over a medium–low heat for 5–7 minutes so that the liquid will have evaporated by the end of this time.

4 Fill bowls with durum wheat. Top with the beans, cavolo nero and tomatoes.

 TIP

If you prefer, you can crumble some Parmesan cheese over the top or add a dollop of soft ricotta cheese to the bowl

VEGAN

KALE

STEAMED CAVOLO NERO

INGREDIENTS

350 g cavolo nero

½ clove garlic

2 tbsp olive oil or coconut oil

Salt and pepper

1 dash lemon juice

HERE'S WHAT TO DO

1 Wash the cavolo nero, cut off the thick stalks and cut the leaves crossways into strips. Peel and finely chop the garlic.

2 Heat the oil in a pan and sauté the garlic until golden. Add the cavolo nero, season with salt and pepper and cook for a short time, stirring constantly. Add 5–6 tablespoons of water and cook for 7–10 minutes over a medium heat. Season with the lemon juice.

 TIP

You can also use this recipe for regular kale. You can give both types of kale a touch of the Orient by sautéing the garlic with 1 finely chopped chilli pepper and by deglazing the pan first with 2 tablespoons of soy sauce and then water. Then sprinkle the cooked leaves with sesame seeds or drizzle with sesame oil.

KALE CRISPS

INGREDIENTS

200 g kale

2 tbsp peanut butter

2 tbsp lime juice

½ tsp sweet paprika

2–3 pinches chilli powder

Salt

HERE'S WHAT TO DO

1   Heat the oven to 120°C (100°C fan). Wash the kale, tear the leaves into small pieces and spin dry. Mix the peanut butter with the lime juice and 5–6 tablespoons of water. Then stir in the paprika, chilli powder and a generous pinch of salt. Add the kale to the paste and knead with your hands.

2   Place the kale pieces on a baking tray lined with baking parchment and dry them out in the oven (middle shelf) for 1 hour–1 hour 15 minutes, using a spoon to detach them from the parchment halfway through. Take the crisps out of the oven, leave to cool and store in an air-tight container.

KALE WITH ORANGE

INGREDIENTS

400 g kale

1 shallot

1 small red chilli pepper

2 oranges

2 tbsp olive oil

Salt and pepper

80 ml vegetable stock

HERE'S WHAT TO DO

1   Wash and shake dry the kale. Cut the leaves off the stems and tear into smaller pieces. Peel and finely dice the shallot. Halve, deseed and finely chop the chilli pepper. Remove the peel and pith from the first orange and cut out the segments from their membranes. Collect the juice. Halve the second orange and squeeze the juice.

2   Heat the oil in a pan and sauté the shallot until golden. Add the chilli and kale and cook for a short time, stirring constantly. Deglaze the pan with just over half the orange juice and season with salt and pepper. Reduce the juice almost completely and then add the stock. Cook, covered, over a medium heat for about 20 minutes, adding the remaining orange juice a little at a time. Towards the end, gently stir in the orange segments and allow them to heat through. Season with salt and pepper.

CRUNCHY
CHICKPEA BOWL

INGREDIENTS

FOR THE SAUCE
2 red or yellow peppers

1 clove garlic

2 tbsp olive oil

½-1 tsp Indian curry paste
(preferably madras)

200 ml vegetable stock

50 g roasted and salted
cashew nuts

Salt and pepper

EXTRAS
Roasted chickpeas
(see p. 52) or see tip

120 g quinoa

1 head baby pak choi (substitute with Chinese mus-
tard leaves or baby salad
leaves)

1 avocado

1 tbsp lemon juice

Nigella seeds, for sprinkling

HERE'S WHAT TO DO

1 Make the roasted chickpeas as shown on page 52.

2 In the meantime, cook the quinoa according to the instructions on the packet. For the sauce, halve, trim, wash
and cut the peppers into pieces. Peel and finely chop the
garlic. Heat the oil in a frying pan and sauté the peppers
with the garlic over a high heat. Stir in the curry paste
and pour in the vegetable stock. Add the cashew nuts.
Cook over a medium heat for 20–25 minutes, stirring occasionally. Drain the peppers and nuts in a colander and
collect the cooking liquid. Blend the peppers and nuts
with just enough of the cooking liquid to keep the sauce
from becoming too runny. Season with salt and pepper
and keep warm.

3 Wash, sort and spin dry the pak choi (or other salad
leaves). Halve and stone the avocado. Scoop out the flesh
with a spoon and cut it lengthways into wedges. Brush
immediately with the lemon juice.

4 Fill bowls with quinoa and drizzle with the sauce. Arrange
the chickpeas, pak choi or salad leaves and avocado on
top. Sprinkle with nigella seeds and serve.

 TIP

If you're in a hurry, simply add chickpeas straight from the tin.

VEGAN

TEX-MEX BOWL

VEGETARIAN

INGREDIENTS

FOR THE SALSA

1 corn on the cob (vacu-
um-packed)

1 small red onion

½ firm avocado

2 tbsp lime juice

2 tbsp chopped coriander

2–3 pinches chilli flakes

Sugar

FOR THE LIME CREAM

½ lime

150 g sour cream

FOR THE TOMATOES

2 firm, ripe tomatoes

1 egg

3 tbsp plain flour

4 tbsp maize flour

⅓ tsp dried oregano

Olive oil, for frying

EXTRAS

1 baked sweet potato (see
p. 106)

120 g rice (preferably long-
grain)

Salt and pepper

Coriander, for garnishing
(optional)

HERE'S WHAT TO DO

1   Bake the sweet potato as shown on page 106. In the meantime, make the salsa. Cook the corn according to the instructions on the packet and leave to cool. Use a knife to cut off the corn kernels from top to bottom. Peel the onion and cut into dice the same size as the corn kernels. Halve, stone and peel the avocado. Cut the flesh into dice the same size as the corn kernels and mix it immediately with the corn, onion, lime juice and coriander. Season with the chilli flakes, 1–2 pinches of sugar, salt and pepper, then leave to stand.

2   Cook the rice according to the instructions on the packet. In the meantime, make the lime cream. Wash the lime under hot water, grate the zest and squeeze the juice. Mix the sour cream with the lemon zest and 2–3 dashes of lime juice. Season with salt and pepper.

3   Wash and cut the tomatoes crossways into thick slices. Soak up their residual water between two sheets of kitchen paper. Beat the egg in a shallow bowl and put the plain flour in another. Put the maize flour in a third. Lightly season the tomato slices with pepper and oregano. Heat plenty of oil in a large non-stick frying pan. First, dust the tomato slices one at a time with plain flour and then dip them in the beaten egg. Finally, coat them in the maize flour, pressing lightly. Fry the tomatoes over a medium heat until golden brown. Take them out and drain on kitchen paper.

4   Take the sweet potato out of the oven, cut it open and scoop out the flesh. Lightly mash it with a fork. Season lightly with salt and pepper. Fill bowls with rice and top with the sweet potato, salsa, tomatoes and lime cream. Optionally, garnish with coriander.

 TIP

For a non-vegetarian version, you can mix 2 tablespoons of grated Parmesan cheese into the maize flour for the tomatoes.

SWEET POTATOES

FRIED

INGREDIENTS

1 sweet potato (about 400 g)

2 tbsp coconut oil

Salt and pepper

2 pinches chilli powder

HERE'S WHAT TO DO

1 Peel and cut the sweet potato into small dice and put them in a steamer basket. Steam the sweet potato over a pan filled with a little water for 10–15 minutes and then pat dry with kitchen paper.

2 Heat the coconut oil in a non-stick frying pan and fry the sweet potato for 5-7 minutes, turning occasionally. Season with salt, pepper and chilli powder.

BAKED

INGREDIENTS

1 sweet potato (300 g)

1 tsp butter or 1 tbsp olive oil

Salt and pepper

HERE'S WHAT TO DO

1 Heat the oven to 200°C (180°C fan). Thoroughly wash the sweet potato and prick it several times all over with a fork. Place it on a baking tray, lined with foil. Bake it in the oven (middle shelf) for about 1 hour 15 minutes, turning once. The sweet potato is cooked when it can be easily pierced with a knife and yields lightly when pressed.

2 Take the sweet potato out of the oven and leave to cool a little. Then cut it open along its length and scoop out the flesh with a spoon. Mash it with a fork and add the butter or olive oil. Season with salt and pepper.

GRILLED

INGREDIENTS

1 sweet potato (about 450 g)

Salt

1 clove garlic

¾ tsp ground cumin

2–3 pinches chilli powder

2 tbsp lime juice

1 tsp maple syrup

3 tbsp olive oil

HERE'S WHAT TO DO

1 Peel the sweet potato and cut it into 2–2 ½-cm cubes. Heat sufficient water in a pan and add salt. Cook the sweet potato over a medium heat for 15–20 minutes. It should be soft (it can be pierced with a sharp knife), but not overcooked or mushy. Drain in a sieve and leave to cool slightly.

2 In the meantime, peel the garlic clove and press through a garlic press. Combine the garlic with the cumin, chilli powder, lime juice, maple syrup and oil and mix well. Coat the sweet potato cubes well in the marinade.

3 Heat the oven grill on the highest setting. Lightly drain off and collect the excess marinade. Place the cubes on a baking tray lined with baking parchment or thread them onto bamboo skewers and place them on the baking parchment. Grill them in the oven (top shelf) for about 10 minutes, turning once or twice, while brushing with the rest of the marinade.

HOT TOFU BOWL

INGREDIENTS

FOR THE SPROUT SALAD

1 large carrot

50 g sprout mix (preferably with alfalfa or radish sprouts)

1 tbsp sesame seeds

3 tbsp freshly squeezed mandarin juice

1 tbsp rice vinegar or white wine vinegar

1 tbsp soy sauce or tamari

1 tbsp toasted sesame oil

FOR THE SWISS CHARD

350 g Swiss chard (preferably rainbow chard)

1 clove garlic

1 piece ginger (10 g)

1 red chilli pepper

2 tbsp sunflower oil

2 tbsp soy sauce or tamari

150 ml vegetable stock

EXTRAS

120 g brown rice

1 small tin (140 g drained weight) kidney beans

Glazed tofu (see p. 111)

HERE'S WHAT TO DO

1 Cook the rice according to the instructions on the packet. Empty the tin of beans into a sieve, rinse under cold water and drain.

2 While the rice is cooking, make the sprout salad. Wash and peel the carrot and use a knife or mandoline to cut it into julienne strips. Put the sprouts in a sieve, rinse well and leave to drain or pat dry with kitchen paper. Toast sesame seeds in a dry frying pan until they release their aroma. Then leave to cool. Mix together the mandarin juice, vinegar, soy sauce and sesame oil. Marinate the carrot in the mixture.

3 Wash and trim the Swiss chard. Cut the stems into about 5-mm-wide strips and the leaves into 1–2-cm-wide strips. Peel and finely chop the garlic and ginger. Halve, deseed and finely chop the chilli pepper. Heat the oil in a wok or a non-stick frying pan and stir-fry the chard stems with the garlic, ginger and chilli over a high heat for 2–3 minutes. Deglaze the pan with soy sauce or tamari, add the stock and cook for 3–5 minutes over medium heat. Then add the chard leaves and wilt them for 2–3 minutes while stirring. Remove the pan from the heat and keep warm.

4 Prepare the tofu as shown on page 111. Mix the sprouts and sesame seeds with the carrot. Fill bowls with rice and top with the sprout salad, chard and tofu.

VEGAN

TOFU

MARINATED

INGREDIENTS

- 200 g tofu
- 1 piece ginger (15 g)
- 1 clove garlic
- 1 red chilli pepper
- 1 stick lemongrass
- Juice of 1 orange
- Juice of ½ lime
- 3 tbsp soy sauce or tamari
- 1 tbsp rice wine (substitute with dry sherry)

HERE'S WHAT TO DO

1 Take the tofu out of the packet and press firmly between sheets of kitchen paper. Then cut into thin slices. Peel the ginger and garlic and finely grate, press through a garlic press or chop as finely as possible. Wash, deseed and finely chop the chilli pepper. Trim off the base and top of the lemongrass. Wash and cut the bottom 10–12-cm section lengthways into thin strips and chop finely.

2 Combine the orange juice, lime juice, soy sauce and rice wine and mix well. Stir in the garlic, ginger, chilli and lemongrass. Transfer the mixture to a resealable freezer bag. Add the tofu and mix well. Seal the bag and marinate for at least 2 hours (6 hours recommended), mixing once or twice if necessary.

 TIP

If you like, you can also pat dry the tofu with kitchen paper and fry it in a griddle pan with a little oil.

GLAZED

INGREDIENTS

200 g tofu

Sunflower oil, for frying

1 clove garlic

1 tbsp maple syrup

1½ tbsp soy sauce or tamari

3 tbsp barbecue sauce
   (shop-bought)

HERE'S WHAT TO DO

1 Take the tofu out of the packet and press firmly between sheets of kitchen paper. Heat plenty of oil in a non-stick frying pan and fry the tofu until it turns crispy and brown. Then leave to drain on kitchen paper.

2 Pour most of the oil out of the pan. Peel and press the garlic through a garlic press and sauté it over a medium heat. Then add the maple syrup, soy sauce, barbecue sauce and 100 ml of water. Stir and reduce over a medium heat until thick and syrupy.

3 Add the tofu to the pan and glaze it for 2–3 minutes, turning several times. The liquid in the pan should be cooked down to a thick and sticky consistency by the end, coating the tofu with a nice shiny glaze.

BAKED

INGREDIENTS

200 g tofu

3 tbsp soy sauce or tamari

1 tbsp rice vinegar or white
   wine vinegar

1 small clove garlic

3 tbsp cornflour

HERE'S WHAT TO DO

1 Press the tofu firmly between sheets of kitchen paper. Then wrap it in kitchen paper, put it into a shallow bowl and weigh it down with a chopping board and a few tins of food. Leave to stand for 6 hours and then pat dry. Cut the tofu into about 1 x 3-cm rectangles. Mix the soy sauce with the vinegar, peel and press the garlic clove and press through a garlic press and combine with the tofu in a resealable freezer bag. Mix well, seal the bag and marinate for 6–12 hours, mixing once or twice.

2 Heat the oven to 200°C (180°C fan). Take the tofu out of the marinade and pat dry. Put the cornflour into a shallow bowl and dust the tofu with a thin coating. Place the tofu on a baking tray lined with baking parchment and bake in the oven (middle shelf) for 30–35 minutes until crispy, turning once or twice.

VEGETARIAN

MATRYOSHKA BOWL

INGREDIENTS

FOR THE CABBAGE

250 g white cabbage

1 small onion

1 tbsp sunflower oil

⅓ tsp caraway seeds

FOR THE HORSE-RADISH SMETANA

120 g smetana (Russian sour cream)

1 tbsp horseradish (shop-bought)

1 bunch chives

FOR THE MUSHROOMS

200 g chestnut mushrooms

1 shallot

2 tbsp sunflower oil

1 tbsp butter

EXTRAS

Salt and pepper

Quick pickled beetroot (see p. 47)

120 g buckwheat bulgur

HERE'S WHAT TO DO

1 Make the pickled beetroot as shown on p. 47 and leave them to steep. In the meantime cook the bulgur according to the instructions on the packet and leave to swell.

2 Wash the cabbage, cut out the hard core as a wedge and slice into thin strips. Peel and halve the onion lengthways and cut into thin strips. Heat the oil in a pan and sauté the onion until golden. Add the cabbage and sauté, stirring constantly, until it begins to brown slightly. Season with the caraway seeds and salt and pepper. Add 5 tablespoons of water and then cook, covered, for about 5 minutes over a medium heat.

3 In the meantime, mix the smetana with the horseradish until smooth. Wash and thinly slice the chives. Set half aside and mix the remainder into the smetana mixture. Season with salt and pepper.

4 Wipe the mushrooms clean and cut into thick slices. Peel and slice the shallot into rings. Heat the oil in a non-stick frying pan and sauté the mushrooms over a high heat for 3–4 minutes until they are lightly browned, seasoning with salt and pepper. Add the shallot and butter to the pan. Cook over a medium heat for 2–3 more minutes until done.

5 Fill bowls with buckwheat bulgur and top with the cabbage, mushrooms and pickled beetroot. Add a dollop of the horseradish smetana. Sprinkle with the remaining chives.

HAPPY BUNNY BOWL

 VEGETARIAN

INGREDIENTS

FOR THE ROASTED CARROTS

1 large, thick red carrot, yellow carrot and orange carrot

½ clove garlic

½ tsp ground cumin

1 tsp ground coriander

2 pinches chilli flakes

1 tbsp runny honey

2 tbsp lemon juice

1 ½ tbsp olive oil

FOR THE CHEESE SAUCE

100 g soft goats' cheese

2 tbsp Greek yoghurt (10% fat)

1 tsp runny honey

2 dashes lemon juice

FOR THE PUNTARELLE

300 g puntarelle (see tip)

½ clove garlic

2 tbsp olive oil

EXTRAS

125 g millet

80 g baby chard

2 tbsp chopped dill

Salt and pepper

HERE'S WHAT TO DO

1 For the roasted carrots, heat the oven to 220°C (200°C fan). Peel and halve the carrots crossways and then quarter them lengthways. Put them into a small ovenproof dish. Peel and slice the garlic. Mix the spices well with the honey, lemon juice and oil and season with salt and pepper. Roast in the oven (middle shelf) for 25–30 minutes.

2 In the meantime, cook the millet according to the instructions on the packet. Sort, wash and spin dry the chard leaves. For the cheese sauce, mix the cheese with the yoghurt until smooth. Season with salt, pepper and the honey and lemon juice.

3 Wash the puntarelle, remove the outer leaves and divide the individual shoots. Halve any large shoots lengthways. Peel and slice the garlic. Heat the oil in a non-stick frying pan and sauté the puntarelle and garlic for 2–3 minutes over a high heat. Then add 3–4 tablespoons of water and cook over a low heat for 3–5 minutes until done.

4 Fill bowls with millet and top with the carrots, puntarelle and cheese sauce. Sprinkle chopped dill over the cheese sauce.

 TIP

Puntarelle is now more commonly found at organic farmers' markets. A member of the chicory family, it consists of thick shoots or flower stems that have a slightly bitter taste and are also good for the digestive system. Naturally, you can always use regular chicory if you can't find any puntarelle.

MUNG DAL BOWL

INGREDIENTS

FOR THE CURRY

80 g dried mung beans

250 ml vegetable stock

1 onion

1 clove garlic

2 tbsp sunflower oil

½ tsp cumin seeds

1 tsp Indian curry paste

1 small tin chopped
    tomatoes (200 g)

2 tbsp chopped coriander

EXTRAS

Kale crisps (see page 101)

150 g quinoa

Salt and pepper

Fried sweet potato (see
    page 106)

60 g baby spinach

HERE'S WHAT TO DO

1 Soak the mung beans in plenty of water overnight.

2 The next day, make the kale crisps as shown on page 101. Drain the beans in a sieve and rinse under cold water. Bring the vegetable stock to the boil in a pan and cook the beans, covered, for 15-20 minutes. They should still be a little firm and not become mushy. Drain into a sieve and collect the stock.

3 Wash the quinoa in a sieve under hot water. Bring 300 ml of salted water to the boil, add the quinoa and simmer, covered, for 25 minutes.

4 Peel and finely chop the onion and garlic. Heat the sunflower oil in a pan and sauté the onion and garlic. Add the cumin seeds and toast until they release their aroma. Add the curry paste and cook for a short time, stirring constantly. Then add the tomatoes and season with salt and pepper and cook, uncovered, over a medium heat for 20 minutes. Add the beans and cook for 10–15 minutes, adding more stock if necessary. Stir in the coriander at the end.

5 Fry the sweet potato as shown on page 106. Sort, wash and spin dry the spinach.

6 Fill bowls with quinoa and top with the mung bean curry, spinach, sweet potato and kale crisps.

VEGAN

JAPAN BOWL WITH MACKEREL

FISH

INGREDIENTS

FOR THE ROASTED AUBERGINE

1 aubergine (about 300 g)

½ clove garlic

1½ tbsp olive oil

FOR THE SAUCE

1 tbsp tahini

2 tbsp white miso paste

1 tbsp soy sauce or tamari

1 tbsp mirin

1–2 dashes chilli sauce (e.g. sriracha; optional)

FOR THE PAK CHOI

3 small heads pak choi

½ clove garlic

2 tbsp sunflower oil

2 tbsp soy sauce or tamari

FOR THE MACKEREL

2 mackerel fillets, skin on (about 160 g)

2 tbsp olive oil

EXTRAS

120 g rice (preferably basmati)

Salt and pepper

1 spring onion

HERE'S WHAT TO DO

1. For the roasted aubergine, wash the aubergine and trim the ends. Halve the aubergine crossways and cut each half lengthways into six wedges. Peel and finely chop the garlic and mix with the oil. Add aubergine pieces, coat well and allow the oil to soak in. In the meantime, heat the oven to 220°C (fan not recommended). Season the aubergine slices with salt and pepper and place on a baking tray lined with baking parchment.
Roast in the oven (middle shelf) for 20–25 minutes until golden brown, turning once or twice.

2. Cook the rice according to the instructions on the packet. In the meantime, trim, wash and slice the spring onions into thin rings. For the sauce, mix all ingredients with 2–3 tablespoons of water until smooth. Optionally, you can add chilli sauce.

3. Wash, trim and halve the pak choi heads lengthways. Peel and slice the garlic. Heat the oil in a frying pan and sear the pak choi on all sides. Season with salt and pepper and drizzle with the soy sauce. Cook, covered, over a medium heat for 3–5 minutes, adding a few tablespoons of water if necessary.

4. Pat dry the mackerel fillets with kitchen paper and season them with salt and pepper. Heat the oil in a non-stick frying pan and fry the fillets on their skin side for 2–3 minutes. Turn them over and fry for another 2–3 minutes until done.

5. Fill bowls with rice and place one mackerel fillet in each. Arrange pak choi and aubergine pieces next to it. Put a dollop of sauce in the middle and sprinkle over everything with spring onion.

TATAKI BOWL

INGREDIENTS

FOR THE PINEAPPLE SALSA

¼ pineapple

½ small red onion

1 small red chilli pepper

2–3 sprigs shiso (perilla, from Oriental food shops)

2 tbsp lime juice

FOR THE TUNA

180 g very fresh tuna fillet (sashimi grade)

½ tsp peppercorns

1 tbsp sesame seeds

2 tbsp olive oil

FOR THE TOPPING

Avocado mayonnaise (see p. 82)

1–2 dashes chilli sauce (e.g. sriracha)

½ red onion

1 yellow pepper

1 punnet shiso cress (substitute with radish sprouts)

EXTRAS

150 g sushi rice (see p. 79)

Salt

HERE'S WHAT TO DO

1 For the salsa, peel the quarter pineapple, remove the core and halve lengthways (you should end up with about 150 g of flesh). Pat dry with kitchen paper and brown the wedges well in a dry frying pan or griddle pan. Leave to cool. In the meantime peel and dice the onion and finely chop the chilli. Wash and shake dry the shiso and pluck and coarsely tear up the leaves. Cut the pineapple into small dice and mix with the chilli, onion, shiso and lime juice. Season with salt and leave to stand.

2 Prepare the sushi rice as shown on page 79. In the meantime, make the avocado mayonnaise as shown on p. 82. Optionally, you can also season it with chilli sauce. Peel and slice the onion into rings. Halve, trim and cut the peppers lengthways into thin strips.

3 Pat dry and season the tuna with salt. Coarsely crush the peppercorns in a mortar and mix with the sesame seeds in a shallow bowl. Coat the tuna in the seasoning mixture, pressing well. Heat the oil in a frying pan. Sear the tuna all over, about 30 seconds for each side. Take it out and cut it into slices.

4 Fill bowls with rice and arrange the pepper, avocado, and onion rings sauce on top. Arrange the tuna slices slightly overlapping. Sprinkle with shiso cress.

 TIP

Raw or cooked? That's a good question. Japanese-style tuna tataki involves searing the outside of the fish, but leaving the inside practically raw. It is typically sliced like sashimi and then dipped in soy sauce before eating.

FISH

FISH

SALMON YAKITORI BOWL

INGREDIENTS

FOR THE SALMON

300 g salmon fillet (as uniform in thickness as possible)

3 ½ tbsp soy sauce or tamari

2 ½ tbsp sugar

2 tbsp dry sherry

1 piece ginger (10 g)

Oil, for griddling

FOR THE CHAR-GRILLED SPRING ONIONS

1 bunch spring onions

2–3 tbsp olive oil

Sea salt

Pepper

EXTRAS

150 g sushi rice (see p. 79)

100 g frozen shelled edamame beans

Salt

Japanese-style pickles (see p. 40)

HERE'S WHAT TO DO

1. Prepare the sushi rice as shown on page 79. Cook the edamame in boiling salted water for 10 minutes and drain in a sieve.

2. In the meantime, pat dry the salmon fillet with kitchen paper. Cut it into 10 uniform cubes and thread them onto bamboo skewers leaving a little space between each cube. Combine the soy sauce, sugar, 4 tablespoons of water and the sherry in a pan. Peel and finely dice ginger and add it to the pan. Bring to the boil and then reduce over a medium heat for 8–10 minutes until syrupy. Brush the sauce all over the salmon cubes and set aside the remainder.

3. For the chargrilled spring onions, wash the spring onions and trim off the base of the bulbs and the tops of the leaves. Then cut them in half crossways. Brush them with oil and lightly season with salt and pepper. Heat a griddle pan and griddle the spring onions for 2 minutes, then turn them over and cook for another 2 minutes. If necessary, you can weigh down the spring onions with a saucepan so that they char well. Season with salt and pepper if necessary.

4. Grease the pan with oil and griddle the salmon skewers on all sides for 6–8 minutes, brushing them with the sauce as often as possible.

5. Fill bowls with rice and top each one with a salmon skewer, edamame, chargrilled spring onions and plenty of the drained pickles.

INDEX

This English language edition published in 2021 by
Grub Street
4 Rainham Close
London
SW11 6SS

Reprinted 2022

Email: food@grubstreet.co.uk
Twitter: @grub_street
Facebook: Grub Street Publishing
Web: www.grubstreet.co.uk

Copyright this English language edition © Grub Street 2021
This translation published by arrangement with
Silke Bruenink Agency, Munich, Germany
First published in German as
Buddha Bowls, Gesund & Bunt – 50 x Energie Aus Der Schüssel
© 2017 Edition Michael Fischer GmbH
Cover design: Michaela Zander
Layout and type: Bernadett Linseisen
Photography: Klaus-Maria Einwanger, Rosenheim

A CIP record for this title is available from the British Library

ISBN 978-1-911667-05-6

Printed and bound by Hussar Books, Poland